C J Holgate was born in England in 1960 and at the age of four, went to Kenya, with her parents. She has lived in Cyprus, Malawi, England and Spain and now she is back in Africa. C J Holgate got a degree in English, music and French at Matlock College, Derbyshire and a Masters in Women's Studies at the University of Barcelona. She has worked as a barmaid, English teacher and gardener. Now she makes jewelry and writes. She lives on her four-acre plot in the Dhuruma farmlands at the Kenya coast with her ten-year-old son, whom she is home schooling. They live with four dogs, four cats, four chickens and a nanny goat.

This book is for you, Cassandra.

C J Holgate

The Mind Boggling Discovery of a Difference

A Love Story

AUSTIN MACAULEY PUBLISHERS™
LONDON • CAMBRIDGE • NEW YORK • SHARJAH

Ordering Information
Quantity sales: Special discounts are available on quantity purchases by corporations, associations, and others. For details, contact the publisher at the address below.

Publisher's Cataloging-in-Publication data
Holgate, C J
The Mind Boggling Discovery of a Difference

ISBN 9781649796929 (Paperback)
ISBN 9781649796936 (ePub e-book)

Library of Congress Control Number: 2023914888

www.austinmacauley.com/us

First Published 2024
Austin Macauley Publishers LLC
40 Wall Street, 33rd Floor, Suite 3302
New York, NY 10005
USA

mail-usa@austinmacauley.com
+1 (646) 5125767

Thanks, Rosa, for wholeheartedly encouraging me to write about us. Thanks, Bem, for being interested. Thanks, Tom and Maggie, for your encouragement. Finally, thanks to anyone who read the drafts and encouraged me, you know who you are. I'd like to thank Chris for reading it, too.

Foreward

For the past twenty-five years I have worked as a researcher and couple counsellor, specializing in the field of intimate relationships when one partner is on the Autism Spectrum. Clara first contacted me in 2009 regarding her suspicions that her partner was on the Autism Spectrum. Clara first approached me in a place of desperation, seeking much needed support and answers regarding her relationship with Rosa. Clara was beginning to question her own sanity, unable to make sense of the reoccurring difficulties that troubled and hindered their relationship. Clara loved her partner very much and wanted to discover why she seemed to be living in a paradoxical world where nothing made sense.

What was different in Clara's case was that her partner was female, she was in a lesbian relationship with a partner who was affected by Asperger's Syndrome. At this time there was very little awareness, both around women on the spectrum, and in particular the impact of neuro-divergence on gay or lesbian relationships. In my work with couples, the majority consisted of heterosexual relationships specifically neurotypical women with men on the Spectrum. It could easily be concluded that the issues affecting heterosexual relationships did not impact the same way on lesbian couples, or relationships when it was the woman on the Spectrum.

At this time little had been published about women on the spectrum and sexuality. Wendy Lawson, (now Wenn Lawson) who is Autistic, was the first to have published the informative and honest account 'Sex, sexuality and the Autism Spectrum' (2005). This ground breaking book offered the reader a much needed insight into the sexuality and the issues facing women on the Spectrum. Lawson's book was highly educational and addressed a very under researched area.

It was this lack of knowledge, information and support that had left Clara feeling so unbelieved and alone. These feelings had prompted her to contact me, in her search for answers to the confusion that clouded her mind in her relationship with Rosa. For Clara, as for many women in neuro-diverse relationships, discovering that her partner is on the Spectrum gave answers to many unanswered questions. Questions that had previously filled her with self-doubt about her judgment and even her own sanity.

This discovery for Clara was the beginning of a journey that she describes with honesty and frankness. Clara's book is one of self-discovery, as she shares her unique journey through life and love, describing openly the up's and down's that she experienced and how she dealt with and sometimes struggled through, the pain that only being in love can bring.

Clara takes the reader by the hand and guides them through her unique experience as a child who grew up in a violent household, a young woman with a spirit of adventure and curiosity, a sexual woman who knows what she is looking for, a loyal lover looking to be loved in return and a lesbian mother whose son is her priority and a continuing binding factor between Rosa and herself.

Clara truly understands the meaning of what it is to be 'Cassandraed' and her book will certainly prove of relevance to the many women and men who find themselves in this situation regardless of whether they are in a lesbian, gay or heterosexual relationship. This is a story of love and hope, based firmly in the reality of what it means to love someone who is on the Autism Spectrum.

Maxine Aston, MSc. Health Psychology
Specializing in Relationships and Autism since 1998

Introduction

In this little book, I talk about what it was like for me to fall in love and live with someone who has what was until recently, called Asperger's syndrome. I didn't want to advise anyone on how to do it or warn anyone against it or provide any contingency plans.

However, since writing it, I have been told that it is more like the story of me, "Lookin" for lurv in all the wrong places. I agree with this. But maybe someone will find the Asperger aspect of it interesting.

It is a memoire of my personal experience and not an objective observation. Every person with Asperger's Syndrome and every Neuro-typical person is different, so obviously my character greatly influenced what occurred between us. I have changed all the names and names of places, to protect our privacy. But I have written as I remember. The order of events is more or less, chronological, but that too depends on my memory. The conversations are an approximation of what we said, again from what I can remember of the mood.

Asperger's syndrome no longer exists, according to psychiatrists. Now it is high functioning autism. I don't care what they call it, but I know it exists and knowing that has helped me to sort out a few mysteries about my life and childhood. The experts, in my opinion are the people who live together with this phenomenon between them, in intimate relationships. They may be spouses or parents or brothers and sisters.

Thinking about it, it could be interesting to hear the other side of this story, Rosa's side. But that will never happen.

I hope you enjoy reading my memoire.

Barcelona

I got off the train in Plaza Catalunya in the middle of Barcelona in October 1992. It was still warm, and traces of the Olympics could be detected throughout the streets, in the form of footprints, showing the way to interesting hangouts and famous buildings. There was an air of celebration and happiness which began to seep through my jaded emotional shield. It seemed like a good place to rest for a while. The guest house I found near Pl Catalunya was nothing special, but it was okay for leaving my rucksack and saddle bag, containing nearly all my worldly goods, while I explored the city.

Two years later, I was still more or less alone. The drinking social life of English teachers didn't provide much sustenance for the soul. But then, I didn't think I had one at that time. I picked up Storm outside La Estacion du Nord, one of the railway stations in Barcelona. She was about two months old. I tucked her into the front of my dungarees and took her to the beach where I was headed to meet some friends. She stepped out onto the beach and walked up and down my back as I lay in the sand. It was winter so we were there to sit and look at the sea, not to swim. Storm was a delicious mixture of tortoise-shell kitten, with a soft white bib. She would travel on my shoulder and come with me for coffee in the bars. I had someone to love at last.

About that time, I was in a bad romance with a pathological but seductive liar. We never appeared on the scene together and everyone except me and the rest of the women she was having sex with, disliked and mistrusted her. Maria was a bit of rough. She dressed like a man and carried it off with her height. But in bed she was soft and feminine with beautiful, large breasts and long, long, brown legs. I firmly ignored the fact that she had lost her two front teeth, it seemed irrelevant. She liked Storm and that was a lot to me.

My friend, Kate, could see that I was in trouble. I had been around her place one afternoon and she could tell I was sad. We had lain down on her bed together and she'd tried to hug me. My body had turned to stone, and I couldn't respond although I liked Katie.

"Cla..." she whispered, "maybe you need to speak to someone, you know, a professional. You seem really unhappy."

"Yeah, maybe..." I stumbled to go on.

I got up a walked out of her house and didn't speak to her again for a long time.

Eventually I phoned that contact, she had given me.

Rosa

I first set eyes on Rosa in a girl's bar in Barcelona in 1996. We started going out together in the winter of 1998. La Selva was the "in" place for any self-respecting, politically active lesbian. Women, looking for a bit of fun, a beer, and conversation would be there. It was tucked away in one of the ubiquitous side streets in Gracia, Barcelona, so you had to know where you were going. La Selva, with its peephole and discreet little sign, was the hub for the out and proud.

I got into the habit of going there after my English classes, at about 10:30. I taught at night schools, and would often drink enough to stumble home afterwards and pass out.

A long, windowless saloon led to a sitting room with a sofa and finally to a narrow little bar. The impression was of a gloomy tunnel. There, we women, spent smoke-filled evenings with the cozy hum of low music in the background. It was a second home to a lot of us. Usually, it smelled of hash too.

There, Blue reigned supreme, the cockney plumber with legs up to her neck, along with Irene, a big, beautiful woman from Navarra, and Carmen a pretty, petite olive-skinned

Catalan. They ran the bar with different styles, each giving the place their own personal flavor.

If Blue was on duty, there was a jovial cocky atmosphere. With Irene, there were always lively political discussions and a good bit of flirting. Noe gave the place an atmosphere of quiet mystery and seduction. There was also Giselle, one French woman, older than the rest and sometimes the bar was hers. Depending on who was there, I was more or less keen to go. Giselle scared the pants off me for some reason. The first time, I went in and sat at a table, she swooped down on me and cooed in my ear, "Yu gut a naym darlin'?"

"Erm yes, I'm Clara."

"Ahhh, Clara, dat is lurvly, can I git yu something sweety?"

Later on, I had an affair with her much younger girlfriend. The girlfriend had another girlfriend who lived in Switzerland and came to visit from time to time.

There was an expression in Barcelona for new faces; *carne fresca* (fresh meat). I heard it once or twice behind my back. I took it as a compliment but was a bit intimidated. Rosa would sometimes sit next to me on a bar stool and smoke joints, silently, while I silently drank lager. Her gentle, undemanding presence relieved and soothed. I was happy not to have to make conversation or feel under pressure to politely, or otherwise, discourage suitors. It was a little strange that she didn't even say hello, but I liked it that way. It was my first memory of Rosa.

Rosa was 39 when I met her. She was a small, dark Spanish woman with Jewish ancestors. She had candid, honey brown eyes looking out from under a long glossy black fringe. Her fine, straight hair was cut short, and she had bushy eyebrows. A small overbite and a large nose gave her face an attractive cheekiness along with a sexy little mole on her jawbone. Her strong hands were ideal for her profession. She was an anesthetist in at Bellvitge General Hospital in Barcelona.

Rosa's small body was perfectly proportioned with just enough feminine curve, to set off her simple sporty clothes and flat shoes.

One evening, I saw her fiddling with something in her lap. Out of the corner of my eye, I could see it was a small piece of paper and a bit of pot. She looked up at me, and said quietly, "Hola, soy Rosa," and pressed the little screw of paper into my hand.

I just stared at her for a moment and then smiled. I wanted to open the tiny missive but decided to wait.

"Gracias," I said and fell silent again.

She looked pleasantly normal and unthreatening in her white T-shirt and dark trouser suit, which turned out to be her work gear. A lot of the women at La Selva were either really butch or very hippy in their dress.

Later, alone my room, I carefully unwrapped the paper to find a tiny piece of pot and Rosa's phone number. I liked her style and put both items into my jewelry box as if they were treasure. I didn't feel under pressure to ring her or even think of her anymore. I vaguely remember seeing her around at lesbian dances and meetings and having the same relaxed and unhurried feeling of being able to enjoy her presence.

One evening, when the bar was lively with billiards and good music, Rosa came up to me with her hands spread out in front of her. She looked intensely into my face, silently inviting me to dance. We didn't speak. Our breasts pressed together, and our bodies touched in delicious places. I felt warm and relaxed and at home in her arms. When the song ended, we separated. I found this unusual but liked the physical closeness without any emotional demands.

We didn't phone or text. In those days, I didn't have a mobile phone. The situation was ideal for me at that moment. Rosa was attractive, mysterious, intelligent and totally undemanding emotionally. She would appear from time to time, like a shadow, flitting around at girlie dances and meetings and greeting me with a grin.

"Hi, what you up to?"

"Oh, not much. Drinking, you know."

"Want a smoke?"

"No thanks."

Rosa looked at me curiously. And I was starting to like her more. Every time we bumped into each other, was fresh. There wasn't any reference to the slow dance. I enjoyed the lightness of our encounters. The need for recognition in other women felt like a burden. If I had had a conversation or a dance with anyone else, they would have wanted to know, what was on the cards. Looking back, I think this freshness came from the Asperger quality of living in the moment.

The Scene

Discos and parties along with political activities and demos were the in thing in 1994, when I first arrived on the Barcelona scene. A monthly bash in some nightclub brought the horniest and best of the Barcelona's out and very proud women, together.

Atmospheres charged with hash, beer and glinting, sassy eyes got my blood pumping with a desire for excitement. It was easy to distinguish between a friend and a flirt, even though we were all the same sex, we all knew. Dani was slugging back the San Miguel's like there was no tomorrow, same as me. We were well on our way to wherever the alcohol and joints would lead us, when Rosa appeared.

"Wanna come and see the snow with me?" It was winter and the Pyrenees were covered.

I looked at her through lager eyes. It was the first time; she had made a direct pass at me, and it was a very unusual one.

"Well…?"

"Why would I want to come and see the snow with you, now?" I grinned at her.

Rosa's face dropped and she walked away. I was in a flirty mood and drunk. Dani tut-tutted.

Years later, I reflected on this. Funny, she should ask me to go to the snow because she disliked walking or anything outdoorsy or adventurous. She had asked purely to seduce me. She had hit on the perfect activity for me. I loved getting into the country.

Lookin for Lurv

The summer of 1997, after the snow invitation, I was recovering from the disastrous relationship with Maria. Staying at my friend Dolors' house, after I had been courteously asked to leave the room, I was renting because of my strange behavior. Using my flat mate's bed when Maria came round had not been appreciated. At Dolors' place, I was trying to sort myself out, seeing my psychoanalyst. A few nice women were making friends with me and seemed interested in a relationship.

Helga, a lovely young German woman, into Gestalt and healthy eating, was pretty. I enjoyed some outings with her but didn't feel the necessary "wow" factor.

We had been shopping for linen clothes together and sat on benches drinking rice milk from the carton.

"So, Clara have you thought about therapy. You know if you're unhappy, it could help." She offered kindly.

"Yep, I already have a therapist. Traditional type. I talk, she listens and says nothing."

"P'raps you need something more active like Gestalt."

"Mmmmm, p'raps, I'll think about it." I drawled lazily.

I hung about at Dolors´ smoking a bit of marijuana and licking my wounds. The marijuana made me laugh a lot and it was a bit like being happy.

Rosa knew where I was and had Dolores' phone number. She rang me.

"Hi!"

"Hello, who's that?" I asked, curious.

"It's me, Rosa…you remember…"

"Oh yes, of course, I remember you. How are you?"

"Doin' okay. How 'bout you?"

"I'm alright, staying here at Dolors´ for a bit."

"I'm thinking of going down the coast this summer, in Josefina, my red Renault Express. Maybe call in to see my pop on the way, he lives in Murcia."

"Mmmmmm sounds nice. But who? What's Josefina?"

"Wanna come along? We could make up a bed in the back of Josephina, my car."

"Tempting, when you thinkin´ of setting off?"

I was starting to get interested. The idea of travelling with Rosa felt like a great escape from the sadness, I was feeling. And she was fresh and different from anyone else, I knew.

"August, probably."

My heart sank a bit.

"My mum's coming over from Hong Kong. I have to be around. Sorry, can't do it."

"Hong Kong's a long way to come! What's she doin' there?" Rosa asked pleasantly.

"My family went there with my stepfather a long time ago. They'd been in Malawi and his job ended. They didn't want to go back to England."

"Well, have a good time with your mum. We'll catch up later sometime, okay?" Rosa's voice sounded unconcerned, but I felt that the invitation for next time was genuine.

"Yeah, really, that would be nice. Thanks for calling."

"You're welcome." Came the casual reply.

The phone call had lightened my mood.

I filled the gaps with an array of people who couldn't ever get close enough to see the ugly pain inside. I had an unusual childhood that left me feeling different and lonely. I was born in 1960, before my parents married. My gran had looked after me, while my mum did university. When I was three, my parents got married and then went to Kenya to teach. My Dad had been violent, lashing out at my mother, my little brother and I. I had once seen him drag my mother across the hallway by her hair. We had moved around a lot and I had got used to saying goodbye to best friends. So many houses and places had left me at a loss to relate to people.

I got involved in a fling that summer with someone camping at a hippy beach up the Cosa Brava. I had taken my mother there. She fitted in marvelously with the laid-back atmosphere.

The affair lasted a month and broke my heart again. Julia charmed me one starry, mediterranean night in a rocky cove where the coolest hippies went to spend their summers. There were tents left there year after year and I was hoping to squat one. I had gone up the coast with Stormy, catching the coastal bus and hitching the last few miles.

The place was a pine and holm oak wood leading down to a little bay of large, round rocks in shades of pink. The rocks were rounded by centuries of rolling in the gentle, sloughing tides. They offered warm, sensuous resting places for bodies fresh out of the salty waves. The crystal clear, fresh sea and the night sky, busy with a million stars had me spellbound. That night was the night of Perseids, the night of thousands of falling stars. It turned out magical and romantic for me.

At the end of the summer of 1997, I was alone again.

Moves

I moved out of Dolors' place into a solitary flat owned by a friend of Luna's. Sweet Luna was doing her best to be my savior and girlfriend. Ten years younger than me and plump and pretty, she wanted to love and care for me. She believed I was a mess and was right. In the end, I felt as if the place wasn't mine and moved into my friend, Dani's girlfriend's house. And into a tiny interior room. It was a beautiful 19th century building, in the Eixample area of Barcelona with a wrought iron lift. Small balconies overlooked the street and on the other side of the flat, an interior patio. Four of us shared the space and I always coveted the rooms with balconies, which I couldn't afford. Susana valued peace and order and there I found peace, friendship and time to concentrate on myself. I was very lonely. Storm saved me every day and every night. And I wasn't getting involved in perilous relationships and situations. The therapist seemed to be helping.

Later, I moved again, with faithful Stormy, who would travel on my shoulders as I carted my belongings on foot and by metro, to my next home. It was another tiny dingy room in a shared house, and I was relieved, when Espe an acquaintance from La Selva and a friend of Rosa, offered me a large room with a little balcony, at her place. Once again, Storm and I upped sticks and moved camp.

The lesbian scene in Barcelona is relatively small, so it's easy to bump into people in unexpected places.

One dreary Sunday afternoon, when I was doing my washing, I walked into the lounge to see Rosa's friendly face smiling at me. My heart warmed just a bit.

As I went through the lounge, collecting my laundry, we smiled at each other, as if we were just acquaintances. But there was a glimmer of recognition in the glance. It wasn't that we were pretending not to know each other. How natural it felt to me to just smile and walk on. I didn't think much about it. Ironically, the emotional distance, so typical of Asperger's Syndrome was just what I needed to be able to get to know someone at that time.

It was spontaneous and typical of moments with Rosa, similar to other experiences of bumping into her over a period of two years since I'd met her. I liked the distance. It was unusual. Most women I'd met in that time had either become friends or disappeared from my life. Rosa was different. She was there and not there. When she was in front of me, her presence was potent. When she was gone, it was as if she didn't exist. This time, she passed me another note with her phone number on.

Soon after that meeting, I got tonsillitis. When I was recovering, Espe who was worried about me, as I didn't see a doctor, called Rosa over. She looked at me and decided there was nothing more to do than take it easy by then. She took me out in her Renault. We ended up on a nudist beach together with no other company. Nudist beaches are blessedly normal, in Spain. And they were, where our crowd usually headed on summer afternoons, autumn evenings and spring mornings. Rosa's lovely body entered my mind, and I was in love. She modestly allowed me to scrutinize every inch of it. She was completely unselfconscious. She told a funny story about a parasol that had been blown away from her on a nudist beach one windy day. She had had to run after it into the bikinis and swimming trunks of the other section of the beach.

She was gentle and concerned about my recovery and I relaxed into her caring. We played naughts and crosses in the sand, sitting very close together. The day was overcast, and I enjoyed the warmth of the soft autumn air without the burning sun. The warm, grey sea lapped gently on the shore reflecting the watery sun's rays. I learned her whole body by sight that day. I let my eyes linger on every detail of her skin tone and shape without once touching her. Her petite body was firm and soft. Lovely breasts and pretty crossed legs lingered on the sand in front of me, inviting but un-anxious. I noticed that her big toe was large and her little toe was tiny. She had a fine bush of black pubic hair and I tried not to stare too hard. Yet once again, the encounter ended with just a goodbye.

I found the women who came on strong intimidating. I couldn't even get to the point of deciding whether I liked them or not. I had clear ideas about what I wanted in a woman physically. Rosa was everything, I liked. Her rather stern, smart clothes belied the breasts, waist and bottom all in the right place. Nice firm legs with some pretty little muscles from her girlish football days had me hooked. I enjoyed the pure sensuality of her unself-conscious nakedness. And she let me do just that.

Limbo

Some months later, I had to move out. Espe's girlfriend was moving in. I shared a house with three others. My tiny bedroom was attached to a living room that one of the flat mates had to pass through to get to the rest of the house. It was another charming Barcelona flat with a huge inner courtyard. I had a tiny balcony again, looking onto that courtyard.

But, long, lonely days and drunken nights were my life. Teaching English as a Foreign Language didn't fill any gaps. I found it hard to connect with people and felt that I had little in common, even with my best friends. They all seemed to me to have important lives with partners, even if they changed periodically. They had meaningful jobs and generally a better quality of life than me. I longed for a partner, but couldn't find the right combination of steady and exciting. The women I went out with were either wildly inappropriate to the point of emotionally dangerous, or boringly nice. That's what I thought. There was sweet, pretty little Luna, who seemed to adore me. I wasn't really attracted to "nice" women but couldn't form a proper relationship with the nasty ones.

The liar had been good in bed but she had pain like me and a lot of other women found comfort in her too. I was one of her harem.

The pretty Luna, did her best to save me. But she couldn't compete with the excitement of emotionally risky relationships. My affair with Maria had been 100% romantic, only in my imagination.

Dating?

Somehow, Rosa gave me a foothold on reality and a touch of excitement at the same time. She was elusive but always somewhere in the background. And she didn't delve into my murky subconscious.

Rosa had a vocation in medicine, she was passionate about being a doctor. She told me, "Ever since I was a little kid, I wanted to be a doctor. Mum bought me a doctor's kit and I got all excited about giving injections."

She asked me for English classes. Working her internship in a big Barcelona city hospital, everyone was expected to have a basic level of English. We would sit grinning at each other over her kitchen table. Rosa's neat attic studio was a single space with kitchen, lounge and bedroom. Her double bed loomed large in one corner of the studio. She seemed less interested in learning English than in setting up a social situation, it was the real "getting to know you" time.

One day I arrived and a strange voice answered to fifth floor doorbell of Rosa's attic flat.

"Holaaaa!"

"Who is it?"

"It's Clara, I've come for Rosa's English class."

"Ahhh."

"Is she there?"

"Yeees, she's here with me…Rooosaaaa!"

"Oh, can I come up."

"Yes, I'll let you in."

It was Rosa's friend and protégé, Gabi. She seemed to be taking on the role of chaperone. As far as I can remember, she left and we did the class. I enjoyed the moments with someone who devoted their entire attention to me. I felt safe and at home and looked after. I don't think Rosa had much money but I charged quite a lot and suspect she had to make a move on me soon as she couldn't afford the English classes forever.

One evening, Gabi was chaperoning us. We went to a concert in one of the lovely old palaces of Barcelona. In an inside patio of one of Barcelona's Eixample, blocks in the open air. Summer was just 'round the corner. Each of these blocks, built on a grid system in the 19th century to cater for the growing city contains a life of its own within the inner courtyard. There were benches and concrete steps to sit on. Rosa's lips were tight and the corners of her eyes squeezed in a bit as she sat down carefully on the hard surface.

"You OK?" I enquired.

"Yeah, my bum hurts a bit, that's all."

"Really!"

"I had a little cyst taken off yesterday, it's still tender."

"My god, you mean they cut it out? Sounds painful!"

Rosa smiled wanly. My eyebrows twitched, and I smirked rather unkindly. Gabi had a poker face. Rosa winced.

I couldn't help feeling turned on. Contemplating her tender backside while listening to the music in the soft spring evening was the most interesting thing I'd done in a while.

We sat through half the concert, until Rosa couldn't take the pain anymore. Apparently, she had been wearing her best Benetton knickers, just in case. She told me later. So many occasions passed when I just didn't get the message of how keen Rosa was.

I had thought that Rosa enjoyed having her friend along. There had been no wink or meaningful glance to hint at anything else.

It was this ease in the encounters, this lack of pressure or even recognition that made it possible for me to keep seeing Rosa, over a period of time. Any sign of impatience or hint that we needed to move faster would have scared me away. Her, not expressing her feelings, calmed me and gave me space to observe my own feelings.

Gandia

Soon after I moved out of Espe's place, Rosa invited me on a trip to Gandia, down the coast. She had friends there and they were having a paella. Gandia is in Valencia, home of this traditional Spanish dish.

Eva another of Rosa's friends from university days, was over from London and was coming along too. Her pals, scattered about the country, had a habit of meeting once a year just to eat together. Eva, a large, flamboyant Spanish woman lived in London with an English man. Her large breasts and jutting chin were the first things, I noticed along with her flounce and enthusiastic laughter at her own jokes. She eyed me suspiciously.

Eva sat in the front of Rosa's van, and I sat in the back, in the middle.

"Clara, you need to sit in the middle."

I raised my eyebrows and cocked my head to one side. "Why?"

"To balance the car. If you sit to one side, the car is unbalanced and it's bad to the suspension.'

We were going down the motorway, not a rough dirt track.

"You're kidding me," I grinned.

At this point, Eva was still and silent.

"No really, if you sit to one side, the car isn't well balanced."

Feeling Eva's warning stillness and seeing Rosa's serious face, I decided not to argue. I was intrigued and still new to Rosa's idiosyncrasies. I wasn't sure whether she was serious or not. But she spent the trip eyeing me in the rear-view mirror.

We arrived five hours later and drove through the campsite gates to the bungalow that Toni and Marc were temporarily occupying their new house was being refurbished. Toni, an elegant 50-year-old with short hair, wore a bikini top, and short shorts, revealing shapely legs. Her face shone with sweat. Marc was completely bald due to alopecia. He was bronzed and only had shorts on, showing off his smooth bronzed muscles. He looked like he didn't work in an office. He was the only one to look me in the eyes and say hello. The others didn't take much notice of me, milling around a camping table. There was Paco and his South American boyfriend. I vaguely remember some tension over him. He wasn't approved of. Then there was another woman and I never found out who she was.

We ate straight from the large, flat paella pan, dipping our forks in. This paella was different from the dishes served up along the beach front in Barcelona. It was greyish in color and had large butter beans in it. It tasted good.

Everyone seemed quite at ease, but I felt awkward, as if everyone was staring at me.

Top priority was to get the lunch served up. We had arrived late. Once we were all sat down, people seemed to notice me.

"So you're Clara," said Toni.

"Yes."

"And you're an English teacher."

"Yes, and I have a beautiful cat." I really wanted to talk about something that I felt passionate about, to show who I was.

"You live in a beautiful house?" The misunderstanding came from the similarity between the two words, in Castilian; *gata* for cat and *casa* for house. My accent wasn't good.

"No, no I have a lovely cat called Storm." I smiled weakly with the sensation that a nice house would have been more acceptable. Toni fell silent.

There was some discussion about the authenticity of butter beans in the dish.

"A proper paella always has butter beans," affirmed Marc.

"Not necessarily," rejoined his wife, Toni.

"The first paellas only had rice and butter beans," chipped in Paco, Rosa's lovely gay friend. During the meal, conversation babbled around me and over my head. Talk about old times and recent events floated on the air. No one took much notice of me, but I was reasonably warmly received.

I felt like they were secretly observing me and quite enjoyed showing that I was worthy of Rosa. I was intensely aware of her presence and her whereabouts. We were still "just friends."

Later in the afternoon, I drifted off for a stroll around the campsite. I felt a bit lonely so when the magnificent Eva appeared nearby, I was happy for the company.

"Hi there, how's it going?"

"Fine, fine thanks, they seem a nice bunch."

"Yes, we've been friends for years, we all know each other very well."

"Yes, I noticed."

"Mmmm, look Clara, Rosa is a lovely person. She's been through a rough time lately."

"Really, she hasn't mentioned anything."

"Well, I don't want to see her get hurt again'"

I gaped, but Eva didn't seem to notice.

"Oh, erm, me neither," I stammered.

With that she turned and walked away, leaving me with a slight frown on my face. I wasn't sure whether to feel flattered or told off. I did feel uneasy. The episode felt a bit too intense. It was the first time I had been openly confronted with the idea that Rosa and I, were an item. I didn't say anything to Rosa.

Moonlight

That night, we stayed at Paco's campsite. It was an impromptu decision. The drive back was too long and it was getting late. I was pleased.

Paco a gentle man in his forties, who had inherited a small fortune, his boyfriend, Fernando, was younger than him and frowned upon by the rest of the group. They were a tight knit group that went back to university days and were jealously protective of each other.

In the moments before bed, an atmosphere of expectation crept in. Everyone sat about, in Paco's living room, "casually." It seemed to me that everyone's attention was on me and Rosa. I knew I wanted to be alone with her.

"So, Rosi, are you staying over?" asked Paco, leaning back comfortably in his armchair with a slight smile of his handsome face.

"I don't mind driving back, we'd get to Barna in the early hours. How 'bout you Eva, d'you need to get back?"

"No, I'm easy if you want to stop over, Rosi."

"Clar, how 'bout you, you want to go home?" Rosa looked at me.

"No, no, whatever you decide, you're the driver." I gave her my best nonchalant look. Then my eyes slid around the room avoiding faces. My ears pricked up like a terrier. What would the verdict be?

"You got any free bungalows, Paco? We could put them up in ours, but it would be a squash.", chimed in Marc. I tensed a bit.

"Already thought of that. I got P2, just the right size for two and another for Eva."

"P2!" Rosa snorted, that's good!" P2 is pronounced *pedos* in Castilian, which means farts. She enjoyed the joke and so did I.

I relaxed a bit as I began to enjoy what was going on. I didn't fancy sharing with people I hardly knew, and I only felt comfortable with Rosa. She was my island in this sea of mystery. These friends were unlike the English people I know. There was hardly any polite conversation. They wanted to know where I was with Rosa and weren't interested in me. I had the feeling that I could join their group if I could fit in, but they wouldn't step out to meet me. Rosa was my port in this choppy sea.
Eva joined us in the cabin. She'd been offered one to herself, but she wanted to be near to Rosa, too. I didn't mind as long as I had a bed with Rosa.

As Rosa tugged off her jeans, I admired her shapely bum. Her blue Benetton knickers emblazoned themselves on my mind, along with the tiny scar from her little operation. I let myself enjoy the delicious, undemanding sensuality of her warm friendly body. She smelt of skin and perfume. We hadn't showered and I drank in her natural scent. I stared at the full moon through the cabin window and content to lie next to her, I drifted off. It didn't occur to me that it was strange that we didn't talk. It was just another part of our unusual courtship, and I liked it. We woke up, still good friends.

Early the next morning, voluptuous Eva bounced into our room from her bunk in living room and onto our bed. She brandished a pink plastic stick.

"I'm ovulating darlings. Isn't it great!"

"Evi!" Muttered Rosa in irritation.

"Really, what does that mean and how do you know." I was pretty ignorant then.

"It means I can have a baby with Rob, I'm in the middle of my cycle!"

"Oohh, I see," I said.

"Yes, I pissed on this stick, and it turned pink, so I'm ovulating."

She bounced a bit more, kneeling just between us and dominating the bed, then retired to her own part of the cabin to get dressed.

The drive home was more awkward than the drive down to Valencia had been. I had a funny feeling that Eva disapproved of me. She exuded a kind of hostile vibe that made me want to get home quick. She chatted to Rosa who was absorbed in her driving and didn't appear to hear her. I tried to chip in.

Eva: "Rob's moved in with me, it took some doing but we finally live together."

Me: "Whereabouts in London do you live?"

Eva: "What? Oh, in Elephant and Castle, you probably don't know London. Anyway, it took me a while to persuade him but no, I think I've got him hooked. I'd like to have a baby quite soon and…"

Me: "I lived in London for two years before coming here."

Eva: "What? Oh really? Yes, well, I think we're together forever now. At least I hope so, I really want to settle."

Me: "Well good luck to you, I hope it works out."

Eva: "Hmmm? Oh of course, it will. Anyway, Rosi you'll have to come over soon and meet him."

I finally settled for looking out the car window. When Rosa dropped me off, she was warm and smiling. Eva didn't really look at me.

Epi

About one month after moving into my new house, Rosa's bit of paper with her phone number on, came to mind and I decided to ring her.

We made a date and met up for a drink. We had a relaxed time with no pressure and sitting in on of the street bars soaking up the warmth of the evening, we smiled quite a lot. The evening ended with us squatting on the steps of one of the many medieval churches.

"So, Clara, tell me about your family, where are they?"

I talked about my brother who has a heroin habit. I can't remember what Rosa talked about.

Another time we went out and sat in a restaurant eating sausage sandwiches with "muchas salchichas." It just means "lots of sausages." Her sandwich had a disproportionate number of sausages in it and she was delighted, like a little girl. We'd giggle about that later, like two children.

The restaurant, down one of Barcelona's back streets, had a blue tiled bar and marble topped tables and ironwork seats. It was art nouveau style, like a lot of the restaurants in Barcelona.

I leaned forward, elbows on the table cupping my chin in my hands. Rosa was busy with a biro and a napkin. I watched her glossy black head and smiled inside. I was where I wanted to be with who I wanted to be with. She was totally absorbed in her task.

She sat in front of me scribbling a spinal cord, glancing up occasionally to see if I was on the same page. I was all agog. In a very short time, she had explained exactly what an epidural was and how to do one. I hadn't even heard the word before. I didn't know that her extraordinary talent at explaining what she was passionate about was a part of her Asperger's Syndrome qualities. At the time, I was on the same page and a couple of pages ahead. My mind unlike hers wasn't 100% focused on her drawing and explanation. I was exploring her face and hair and hands appreciatively.

Romance

Toward the end of October, when the summer heat still infused the musty, old streets. We ambled along one evening chatting. We stopped on the street corner where there are low stone buttresses well worn by a couple of centuries of carts brushing past. The buttresses protected the corners of the houses in the olden days. We kissed for the first time and she asked me up for a coffee. I never drank coffee at night. But that seemed irrelevant. We became lovers as well as friends in her little attic flat.

We had arrived at her 5th floor flat without lift at a run. There wasn't any coffee. We had undressed ourselves and leapt only her double bed. The feel of her warm skin was rich and comforting. We didn't look lovingly into each other's eyes, like at the pictures and that was liberating. She went down on me, only occasionally glancing up to look at my face. She cared about me. She brought me to orgasm and then let me sleep. I had had sex with quite a lot of people but hadn't had an orgasm with anyone.

Rosa's relaxed detachment relaxed me. It felt like coming home.

I was on an "in love high." She had to get up early to go to work the next morning. I stayed in her bed. The English classes I taught in private academies, classes were in the evening.

I had got some good loving from Rosa that night.

She was extraordinary. I adored her delight in me and life was sweet when we were alone together.

Her bathroom was small, and her bath was too. We'd bath together and shriek, as we came and then laugh a lot. I enjoyed a gay abandon in sex that was new to me.

But when Rosa turned off, the laughter stopped short.

Plaza Espana

We'd been together about two weeks when Rosa stood me up for the first time. We'd arranged to meet near my work one evening. I was an English teacher and taught evenings until 10 pm. We were to meet at Plaza España.

I waited there for an hour before giving up. I was insecure anyway and this set my warning bells jingling deafeningly. But instead of putting me off, it played on my insecurity. It was like a red rag to a bull and I couldn't give up.

Neither could I think clearly about what to do so I rang Katie for help.

"Katie!"

"Hi Clara honey how's it going, where's that girl of yours?"

"She's stood me up."

"You sure she's not just late, she's Spanish, you know."

"I've been here an hour!"

"Where?"

"Plaza Espana."

"Yuk, not a nice place."

Plaza Espana was basically a huge roundabout on the outer part of the inner city. There was an exhibition center there but at nights it was deserted and depressing except when the magic fountains were playing every Saturday night.

"She's probably in La Selva, maybe she got the wrong place. She hasn't rung?"

"No, nothing but I think I'll go to La Selva anyway, at least I can get a drink."

"Good girl, let me how it goes."

I went straight there and found her. She explained, beaming, that she'd been looking for a car and time had slipped by, and she'd missed her appointment with me and that she was delighted to finally see me. I listened, my eyes widening inside my head but not on my face. There were other people there listening, but it seemed that I was the only one to find all this strange. Maybe it was a Spanish thing not to turn up to dates and then, not apologize. The concoction of feelings inside was interesting. I was glad to see Rosa. I was glad she was glad to see me. I was tired and sad that she hadn't turned up and I was scared because all this seemed normal to everyone except me.

I tried to make sense of it and gave up and gave in to Rosa's grinning face.

"Aw Clar I was up in Pedralbes looking at cars to buy. Completely forgot the time and when I remembered, my mobile had run out of juice."

"I was waiting an hour."

"Yeah, well I'm really sorry, okay."

"At Pl Espana."

"Alright, I said I was sorry."

"Did you think it would just be okay?"

"Dunno, I thought you'd come here."

I gave up. Rosa's grin looked as though it might fade if I carried on. I slumped on the bar stool and ordered a beer. We went back to Rosa's place later.

Birthday

Rosa's birthday was just before a trip that she was planning to New York. This trip was her treat to herself, and she was going to hunt down a particular professor to direct her thesis on POMC (proopiomelanocortin). This hormone takes care of injuries and illnesses. The woman Pilar wanted, was the sole expert in the 1990s.

The women at La Illa were planning a surprise party for her. Rosa and I were the talk of the town as the new couple, and I was to be and hostess with the mostest. I felt a little unsure about all this, as something was telling me not to jump the gun with this girl. We'd only been going out for a month. Everything felt unsteady. We liked each other but were looking in different directions. I gazed toward the future and Rosa to the past. She had what seemed an endless list of exes and a couple of not-too-loose ends.

I felt like I was in competition with Gabi for Rosa's attention.

"Um…Gabi…You know La Selva?"

"Course I do, I go there with Rosa, you know."

I shuffled my feet a bit, feeling the point in the remark.

"Well…erm…we're having a party for Rosa. Wanna come along?"

Gabi stared at me with a little sneer. "Mmmmm," she managed and walked away.

I sighed and asked myself if I'd ever get it right with Gabi. Actually, I wanted to smack her in the face and tell Rosa how nasty she'd been. But I recognized that the feeling came from my own confusion about their relationship.

Later, Rosa told me that she had asked Gabi if she wanted to live with her. Gabi hadn't wanted to. Rosa explained that there was no sexual attraction, just a kind of dependency. Gabi leaned on her as a kind of protector and had all her drinks paid for when they went out.

There was the work "do." I tagged along with Rosa, Gabi and a couple of other workmates in the know and there was the lesbian bash at the bar in which we were officially celebrated as a couple. The whole thing felt a little unreal. I didn't feel whole heartedly exuberant about anything. I didn't fit in at either of these parties.

It was clear that her workmates weren't into me. The ground was rocky, but Rosa was charismatic and charming when she wanted to be and very sexy. She seemed oblivious to my discomfort, and I didn't want to spoil things by raining on her parade. Warm greetings and animated conversations babbled around me. I got the formal two cheek kiss and quick introduction.

"Hi I'm, Suzi delighted to meet you."

"Hi I'm, Clara, me too."

"Rosi, Happy Birthday darling!"

"Thank-you sweetie, it's the big 40 now. I love that number, so rounded."

"Yes, you're a big girl now. So, how's your day been?"

Rosa was oblivious to my discomfort. The restaurant was the "Pescaditos" (Little Fishes). An ornate art nouveau building. It had the slightly rancid odor of old Barcelona. It's stones had probably seen 1000 years of city life. The dimly lit cavernous dining room was decorated with tile pictures and old-fashioned lamps on the walls. The pica-pica that the group had ordered filled the table and we all helped ourselves to what we fancied. Anchovies, anchovies in vinegar, cheeses, cold meats, olives and pan amb tomacat (huge slices of crusty farmhouse bread smeared with crushed tomatoe and olive oil and garlic, made my mouth water. I worried about the price. This was an expensive place, and I wasn't well-off. It turned out that Rosa treated everyone. It's the custom in Spain for the birthday person to treat everyone.

I looked on as everyone talked shop. Rosa didn't glance my way and I crumpled into my seat and longed for the evening to end. I was out of my depth with what felt like rudeness and Rosa was in another dimension. She couldn't help.

"Oh my God," chirped Suzi, "did you see Gabriel today. Seems he's been made head of eyes."

"Hell yes," came a reply from someone, "he's all over himself. I keep out of his way these days."

"I'm going down to Valencia," announced Aurora.

"What permanent?" asked Rosa.

"Yeah, I've been offered a good position down there and Vicente is down there too."

"I'll miss you in the theatre," said Rosa.

The evening dragged painfully on and there was no respite when I finally got Rosa alone.

"I was miserable this evening."

"Why?"

"No one talked to me, and you just ignored me."

"No, I didn't, I was just talking to my friends."

"I felt lonely."

"Well don't come next time."

I stared at her, unable to make sense of what she was saying, maybe she was being facetious or nasty, but her face was dead pan.

"Do you really mean that?"

"Yes, you didn't like it so don't come next time. I don't mind."

I shrank at the idea and a sense of hopelessness broke over me like a big wave. It was unbearable, so I continued to argue.

"But that's not fair."

"Why not?"

"It means I can't share your friends."

"If you don't like them, why do you want to share them?"

Her logic was startling and impeccable, and her fixed stare told me to back off. I slunk off thinking about psychologists and solutions.

I felt disappointed and let down by both Rosa and by myself. I wasn't used to falling short in social situations and considered myself to be something of an expert in getting on with people, initially. Failure in friendships usually came later.

The contrast between the soft fingers on my face and gentle passionate kisses when we were alone and the cold, narrowing eyes when we were out with her friends, was astonishing. I was enthralled with Rosa. It was a heady but painful attraction. It suited me in a way. It kept me on my toes.

Sex

Love making was lovely, to the point and sensitive. She caressed me with strong, caring hands and her firm touch relaxed me. I could rely on her to give me pleasure. She liked seeing me satisfied and put all her attention into loving me. And I loved to watch her come. We didn't do a lot of talking.

"You're gorgeous…" Rosa grinned, sitting astride my stomach, looking down at me.

"Thanks. I love your breasts."

"Nice, aren't they. One of my best features. Won a beautiful breast competition with them once."

"Yeah right, ha, ha."

"Really, I'm not joking. When I was a teenager, we had a competition in our girls' football team."

"And you won!"

"Yep," she smiled.

I could rely on Rosa to give me pleasure. She didn't use body lotions because the texture and smell of them bothered her. I enjoyed the natural scents of her body and the silky feel of her hair and I loved the sensation of leisure. I had known Rosa for a long time before going to bed with her. I stared at her body long and hard daring to possess it.

She puzzled me sometimes.

"You never say no."

"Why would I, I like you."

She just smiled and carried on kissing me.

Rosa understood sex and knew how to approach it. It was one of her interests. There were a few basic rules, which I didn't mind at all. In fact, I rather liked the comfort of knowing what to expect.

I wasn't to touch her nipples as her milk ducts were always open. It was something to do with her hormones and if bacteria got in there, they could get infected and sore very easily. I thought she was having me on at first, until she showed me a liquid that came out of her nipples when she squeezed them. It was very intimate and a turn on, having limits. She didn't like to experiment with her own body much. I was surprised when she didn't enjoy penetration. I had come from a world where that was the end game in sex. Even on the lesbian scene, the women talked about it with bravado. There were conversations about how, by whom, with what and up to where. I got a small dildo, but we didn't share it.

I didn't notice how specific her sexual desires were, at first. I was busy getting my own wants sorted out. Little by little, I learned some guidelines. She liked firm gentle touches and simple orgasms.

We had gone down to Almeria in her red Renault and parked on a beach. Sleeping in a van on a beach in Southern Spain, with a new girlfriend, was, by definition romantic. As close to my romantic dreams as I had ever come by the age of 39. I was feeling very sexy and romantic and started to play. Massaging her clitoris until she nearly came and then slowing down, I began to trail my hands between her thighs and buttocks. Rosa sighed heavily and turned her back on me. I tentatively tapped her on the shoulder.

"What's up, what've I done?"

"Oh nuthin, nuthin."

"Come on, something's up."

"Why did you stop?"

"I was trying to keep it going longer, I was teasing you."

"Well, you turned me right off."

"Oh, sorry."

"It's OK but I don't like that, don't do it again."

"Mm, well, OK."

Shrinking inside, I clung to her back, waiting for her to turn round and hug me. Instead, she fell asleep. Tears squeezing through my tightly closed lids, I buried my head in her nape.

For me, it was a marker in our sex life. I learned some boundaries. My attempts at being the big seductress had flopped like a bad meringue.

Valladolid

There was one last birthday celebration for Rosa. She wanted to go to Valladolid, her home city, to celebrate. Valladolid is situated in the middle of the flatlands of Castile. It's the ancient capital and it's from there that Isabel la Catolica sent Christopher Columbus off to discover the Americas. The city is crammed with pristine medieval buildings and steeped in monarchic Spanish history. Going there is like stepping back in time, not only because of the buildings. The people seem to come from another era, perhaps Franco's time. Everyone is dressed in the same style and on a certain day in autumn, every woman decides it's cold and gets out her real fur coat.

Valladolid is known for a couple of other things. The vintners produce probably the least known but best wines in the world. It also has a lot of sheep. Rosa's celebrations would consist of choosing a live lamb, roasting it and eating it with lettuce leaves and excellent wine. The lettuce leaves were always a half-hearted nod at including something green in the meal. No one took vegetables seriously in Valladolid.

Rosa invited me along, but I felt too remote from her world and too green in the relationship to plunge into her world.

I phoned her. "Hey how are ya."

"Great, I chose my lamb today."

"What?"

"I chose the lamb for my party."

"Oh, you went to the butchers?"

"No, I went to the farm."

"You choose a live baby lamb to roast!"

"Yeah, it's what we do here. Delicious, especially the little ribs."

"Wasn't that hard? You love animals."

I was taken aback by her casual way of telling me and wondered why she hadn't mentioned this tradition before going there. For me, it was quite a revelation. I didn't feel disgusted. I eat meat and know the score with supermarket stuff. I reckoned if the lamb had at least seen daylight, it had had a decent start.

"I know but it's just what they do here."

"Don't think I could eat a lamb that I'd seen with its mum."

"It's just what we do. We're preparing the house."

"Is there a lot to do?"

"Yes, and it's chaos. The oven's broken and Vero is sooo disorganized."

They were having the feast in Rosa's older friend, Vero's house. This woman had looked out for Rosa when her mother died young, and she was only 18.

"Thank goodness Felix is here to fix things up."

Names of people had never met came at me as I tried to imagine the scenario. A broken oven, a disorganized hostess and a whole lamb to roast, it didn't sound fun to me. But Rosa was in high spirits, amongst her own people.

"Okay well enjoy yourself."

"Thanks, bye."

I missed Rosa but had a funny feeling that I had done the right thing in not going. She was doing something that I wouldn't enjoy but I wished her all the best.

New York

The little woman I had got involved with was a Pandora's box of surprises. News of a trip to New York came in dribs and drabs. She was going for a week, in search of an elusive professor, expert in genetics. Rosa was doing a thesis on POMC (Pro-opiomelanocortin) and the genetics of pain and healing. She wanted this woman who was the only other expert in the field, to direct her.

It was Rosa's own 40th birthday treat to herself and the last in her parade of celebrations. I was hazy about what was happening in New York. Bad communication was one of our characteristics. At the beginning with Rosa, I just accepted ragged explanations and put it down to us being new to each other. Culture differences also gave a feeling of not knowing what was going on, a lot of the time.

I was very much in love. But I knew that the relationship was new and didn't mind being separated. I did have an uncomfortable feeling of separation on a sentimental level. We didn't discuss it.

Glamorous Gabi seemed all of a flutter. Wasn't I terribly worried about Rosa going to New York all alone. I tried to look her in the eye she seemed to be avoiding me.

"Well, no, not really," I replied.

Gabi gave a tiny snort and pursed her pretty lips. But the conversation had started a faint trail of wispy anxiety floating around in my brain. Did I need to worry about something that wasn't Rosa going to New York? Something less tangible?

There was a gulf between the warmth and comfort of being alone with Rosa and the loneliness when others were around. Sometimes I felt I'd dreamed up the whole relationship. There was me and Rosa and then there was the rest of the world and the three didn't fit comfortably together.

Rosa had stayed at the "Banana Bungalow," in downtown Manhattan, for four nights. She found her professor very quickly. They'd talked and Professor Castellanos agreed to direct the thesis.

Rosa also had some other adventures in New York. She explained these in a garbled phone call.

"I found a drunk drowning, in his own vomit."

"Really? Where?"

"On the steps of the hostel, I can't speak English, I didn't know what to do."

"So, what did you do?"

"I phoned Valery in Miami."

"Miami? Who's Valery?"

"She's my friend from Valladolid."

"So why is she in Miami? And why did you phone her?"

"She moved there with her husband; they have a little girl now."

"OK and why phone her."

"To talk to the hostel manager and get an ambulance for this guy."

She helped the drunk and Valery paid for an airline ticket for Rosa, to go down to Miami and see her. My mind was spinning by the time Rosa got back. But she was very loving and had bought me little gifts, so I put my confusion to the back of my mind. She was excited and tender and distant all at the same time. Her mind seemed to be still in New York. But she seemed happy to see me. During her time in New York, I had slept in her flat, to feel close to her. I wasn't sure if it was wise but Dani, our champion assured me, "She'll be made up to find you in her home Clar." So, I stayed there to wait for her. She didn't talk much about her feelings or her experiences in the Big Apple. I would have liked to have had a special welcome back celebration. But that didn't happen either. She was indeed pleased to find me in her home.

Little Mysteries

Early on in our liaison, Rosa began to reveal to me tit bits about her ancestry. I didn't believe her. I thought she was either joking or trying to impress me or that I'd misunderstood.

Her great, great, great grandfather had been physician to the king at the time. He had invented a way to cure the king's backaches by suspending him from the beams for a certain length of time and letting his vertebrae click into place again.

Everything about Rosa was new and exotic to me so I listened, wondering who I had got involved with.

Her mother was a minor marquise but had fallen into poverty and if Rosa wanted her title, she'd have had to pay for it. Her mother had been one of the teachers who went out to remote regions during the republic. When Franco was in power, she's continued teaching in a small town in central Spain. There were streets in Valladolid named after her ancestors. They had been Jews who had married into the royal family to save their skins, when Isabel la Catolica had carried out her scourge of Jews and Arabs throughout Spain. There was haemophilia in her family, and she hadn't had a baby because of it. Her great grandfather had made a series of priceless cartoons about his life. She showed me these gems. She had been the only one to preserve them when her mother had died. Her brothers weren't interested in them. Her mother was delighted to have healthy strong boys. It was an extra blessing because of the haemophilia in the family. One of her cousins had died of it.

She gave me this information in the same disorderly way as I have written it. It was usually delivered as part of a conversation about mundane, everyday life. I felt like I was in some kind of time warp, sometimes. The stories she told me were worthy of more ceremony. Maybe something like, "Would you like me to tell you a little story about my ancestors?"

We would be talking about her day in the hospital, maybe someone had had a backache. Rosa would chime in.

"Yes, and my great, great, great grandfather found the solution to king's back problem. The king had a bad back from riding."

"Who? What? Is this a family joke?"

"Nooo, really, my great, great…"

And she elaborated on her true story.

39

My birthday was on the 5th of December, about two weeks after Pilar's New York trip, I was going to be 39. I was looking forward to something special too, because this new relationship felt like it was important. I had spent a lot of lonely birthdays and I had high hopes for this one. New lover, new life. "Happy birthday, darling!" Rosa said early that morning. It was a weekend and we were together, no ´guardia´, (24 hour hospital shift).

"Mmmm, thanks," I mumbled back, sleepily and turned over to snuggle down for a while.

I hadn't planned anything either, leaving it in Rosa's hands. I just relaxed and enjoyed the warmth.

After snoozing a bit longer, I got up for some off Rosa's delicious filter coffee and breakfast. We lay about watching telly and enjoyed the quiet company for a while. Then I began to wonder what the plan was. It dawned on me little by little that there wasn't any plan. There was a "Guia del Ocio," the comprehensive, weekly entertainment guide for Barcelona. I bought it every week, mainly for the cinema. Flicking through the theatre section, I began to feel more and more agitated as Rosa continued to watch telly, completely oblivious to my fussing.

"So er, have we any plans for today?"

"Mmm? No, why?"

"It's my birthday, I thought you might have a plan."

"No, I hadn't thought of anything."

"Can we go to a theatre I love the theatre."

By then, I felt disappointed and hurt that she hadn't thought my birthday important enough to do something special. But I soldiered on.

"We can catch an afternoon show and be back early."

"It's freezing out there and I'm okay here, I don't need to go out."

She went to the sink to wash up. I remembered all her birthday shindigs and wondered what was happening here. I stood there rooted to the spot, willing her to take notice. She flitted about the flat tidying up.

"Can we at least go out for a walk I feel like some fresh air."

Her back at the sink said, "Leave me alone."

"Please, Rosa, I feel a bit miserable if we don't do anything. I'm not used to celebrating my birthday, but I thought it might be special with you."

"I've got a bottle of cava (Catalan champagne)."

"Why didn't you say?"

"You didn't ask!"

"Well let's go down to the sea and drink it on the beach."

"Well, alright, if you really want to."

I sat up and smiled at her. "Great I'll get my jacket."

On the way down to the sea through the Barcelona streets, we met Katie. She eyed us curiously.

"So, what you two up to? It's your birthday isn't it, Clara? Had a nice day?"

"Lovely,"

"Mmmm, I see, so what have you been up to?"

"Well, we've been cozy at home and now we're off down to the beach with this bottle of Cava."

Katie looked questioningly at me. Her eyes darted back and forth from Rosa and me. She looked like she wanted to say something but gave me a little hug instead.

"We just decided to be quiet and romantic, and Rosa has bought a bottle of cava."

"Right, well, enjoy yourselves," she said looking hard at Rosa.

I had tried to make our walk along the prom sound like all I wanted to do in the world. I was mortified at having been found out. We'd been together a month.

We walked along the seafront in the early December evening. The sky was overcast and the sea a grizzly grey color. Rosa cradled the cava and I trotted along beside her.

We should have been connecting but we weren't. The place we connected best was alone, in bed or doing routine things at her flat. Then there were no conflicts and no issues to discuss or any timetables to comply to or any third parties to accommodate. If Rosa wanted my attention, she could be all ears. Right now, she was irritated.

"So, tell me about yourself," she demanded out of the blue.

"Erm, I'm 39 today. I live in Barcelona with my cat Stormy and I'm going out with Rosa Buenaventura."

"More, tell me more."

"I came to Barcelona by chance after working in a campsite in France over the summer: I was going to go back to England and do a PGCE, but I decided to come here instead to learn Spanish. That was in 1992. I was going to offer French and Spanish for primary and I didn't speak any Spanish although I knew the grammar."

"Mmm, did you see that egret, it's on its way to Gava."

"How d'you know?"

"Gava's down that way. Let's open this cava."

We sat on a dune looking out over the sea. The chiringuitos, that were lively with people all summer, serving drinks and food, were all closed now.

Split

The day after my birthday, we split up. It was Sunday and Rosa had arranged to help a friend move house without telling me. I complained too much, and she dumped me. That was how it seemed to me.

That Sunday afternoon, Rosa announced that she was helping Susana, a friend of hers, to move house with her van. She told me that I could hang out or go home. I had been lulled into a cozy romantic feeling again. Rosa's flat was like a little nest where time stood still, and the outside world stayed still. I had expected to have her to myself. I was shocked out of my bliss by Rosa's abrupt announcement. It made me angry and frustrated and I couldn't keep it in.

"Why didn't you mention this before?"

"Didn't think it was important."

"Where's her flat, how are you going to carry the stuff? When are you going?"

"I'm going now, you can come if you want."

"And if I don't want to come?"

"Stay here."

I couldn't believe her coldness. I had a bad feeling. She avoided eye contact, as she often did when bothered, and mumbled her replies.

It wasn't so much the fact of Rosa helping a friend that made me mad. She hadn't mentioned anything about it. The day before had been my birthday and there hadn't been a plan. Today the day after, she had a big plan. I felt hopelessly jealous.

I was confused. Helping a friend seemed perfectly nice and normal. It was the way in which Rosa delivered the ultimatum that I couldn't stomach. That was the problem with a lot of what Rosa did. It was always quite nice but her way approaching me was dismissive. It made it seem to me as if I wasn't important.

I went along with a long face and had an awful time. Susana asked what was up. I told her Rosa wasn't being nice to me. She said, "Yep, Rosa can be a bit like that sometimes."

Afterwards, we had a brief argument and then she took me to a viewpoint looking out over the city. It should have been romantic. Under the circumstances, it was just alarming. I wanted to talk about what was happening and Rosa had completely clammed up. I felt like she was taking me to the site of execution. I wanted to be with her but didn't understand her silence or why she wanted to take me to this place where lovers looked over the city, when we were clearly at loggerheads.

I fiddled with stuff in the car and caught her giving me sidelong glances. I laid hands on a spare "panty liner" that she had in the door pocket and waved it about bit with a silly smile.

"Turn you on, does it?"

"Yes."

It was another quirky moment and we laughed. But I hunkered down in my seat and jammed my hands into my coat pockets. A grey feeling of loneliness came over me. It was as if I had imagined any connection, we'd had. I wanted to talk. Rosa shut down.

In the end, we went down to the city again. She asked where I wanted to be dropped.

I can still remember the expression on her face as I looked back after she had left me near my friend Jane's house. Her features were set in stone. There was no regret or warmth or any kind of apology.

I now understand that expression better and have seen it innumerable times and know that it is just a blank which meant that her mind had shut down. What I read as icy coldness was unintentional. There was no particular message.

Looking back, I think she hadn't planned to split up. But she didn't know how to handle the conflict and I was too scared of losing her to think straight and question what was happening. For her, it was a case of fight or flight, and she flew, leaving me stunned.

I was miserable and gave myself the blame for being too needy. I dragged my feet to Jane's place. My home was too near to a different reality at that moment, and I didn't want to know about it. Everything had happened so fast. The love affair, the disagreement and the split, all in the space of a month.

Jane's shoulder was warm and comforting and non-judgmental. She made tea and we drank the hot liquid in amicable silence. Jane was single and would have liked a boyfriend. But she didn't talk about it much. She was a conscientious English teacher. But her heart was in her art and her love of the color blue. With a twinkle in her cool blue eyes and a little smile on her wide generous mouth, she got out some colors and paper. "Art therapy, Clara." I calmed down a bit and walked home through a very bleak Barcelona.

I couldn't forget her. It had seemed so nice and gentle at first and that had been how I'd liked it. I couldn't believe that I had failed again. I had been on my own for a while, seeing an analyst and felt like I was finding myself and learning to like myself. I thought I was ready for a good relationship, and it had seemed that Rosa was nice with a bit of spice. The problem was the information gaps, but I didn't know that.

I believed the split had come from something serious and took it seriously. But there was an itch that I had to scratch and couldn't just let it be.

In Between

In the meantime, I discussed it with gentle Scot Jane. She was the artist with sparkling blue eyes and milky Scottish skin. She was an artist in every sense. She drew beautiful sensitive portraits and then lucid abstract blue landscapes inspired by her home. She had a magic studio in the Poble Nou, a neighborhood in Barcelona, originally a neighbourhood of warehouses and industry. The old warehouses were now flats and studios. Her's was a section of a huge, high roofed hall, divided up with metal panels. She had all her paints and creations there.

The place looked grim from the outside. But as I went inside the door, an array of artists' spaces opened out into a wonderland. The few people there, smiled greetings and I felt like I'd been invited into Aladdin's cave.

Jane's art therapy was free and fun. We'd go to the studio, Jane in her ample overalls, her loose T-shirt slipping off her pretty rounded shoulder. Her delicious, cheeky smile invited me to splash around with her paints while she created masterpieces next to me. She also provided therapy in the shape of macaroni cheese dinners with wine.

This gentle company soothed my anxiety and gave me space to think. The great thing was that we didn't talk much about Rosa and that gave me space to reflect.

I realized that there was something strange going on. I was curious to find out what. I had a feeling that the incident with Rosa was big, but at the same time meaningless. There was something that I wasn't getting. I was fascinated and didn't want to let go.

I talked it out of myself with my analyst and realized that deep down, I didn't think it was over with Rosa. I couldn't explain it rationally because she hadn't rung or made contact again. I just felt that there was more to the affair than met my eye.

Christmas

Something niggled at the back of my mind. I couldn't let go. I knew that Rosa had been serious when she had dropped me off that last day. But it didn't make any sense in the context of what had gone before. One minute she had been passionate and devoted and the next it was over.

As I talked it all out with my analyst, I realized that there was something very strange going on and was still curious to find out what. The feeling was that this incident was big but at the same time little and meaningless. It was very odd, as if there had been a gap or space and something had gone on that I couldn't see, as if some important information was missing. If I made an effort, I could fill the gap and fix things. It was hurtful but at the same time fascinating.

Just in time for the girls' Christmas bash in La Illa. Janie took me clothes shopping. I obtained some super-duper, indigo velvet pants and a white cotton shirt.

I expected Rosa to be there at Christmas. Everyone who didn't go home to their families, hung out at La Illa. We were known as the Christmas orphans. I thought that if I behaved as if nothing had happened and I wasn't at all upset, maybe Rosa would take a second chance on me. She had seemed pretty keen before. I just had a feeling that it wasn't quite over.

It was the "Caga Tio" party, a Catalan custom dating back to before Christianity. There was a time when nature ruled supreme and people who worked the land, celebrated every year in winter. I don't think the Christmas celebrations included the birth of Christ because the Catar religion was quite different to the Catholic tradition. They cover a log with a blanket and put a face on one end of it. They then gather around and whack the log hard with sturdy sticks. They chant;

"Tio, tio caga torro,

Si no ens tens mes, caga diners,

Si no en tens prou,

Caga un ou."

Roughly translated as,

"Uncle, uncle shit some candy,

If you haven't any more shit some Money,

If you haven't enough, then shit us an egg."

Nowadays, sweets and small gifts are hidden under the blanket and after each round, someone puts a hand under and fishes something out.

We all bashed happily at the log, clutching beers and laughing raucously. My eyes searched for Rosa's and found her smiling at me. It seemed like nothing had happened between us and everything was fresh and new again, just like in the 'getting to know you time'. We were back together.

When I asked Rosa about our first split, to find out how she had felt, she reacted as though nothing had happened between us. She explained that she had had a lot on her mind that month and she had had to take care of her stepmother, who had been visiting Barcelona. She apologized briefly for not seeing me for a while. At the time, she had said nothing about her stepmother's visit.

I remember her bringing me an old telly off the street as a gift. It wasn't my dream present, but I was amused to see her climbing the stairs to the flat where I had a room with an old telly on her shoulder, she was obviously very proud of it. Later she bought me a CD player for Reyes, the Three Kings Christmas celebration in Spain, when children traditionally received gifts. I think she was setting me up comfortably, as she would have liked to be set up. She bought me some sheets for my bed too and was clearly trying to take good care of me.

Jumble

The English lesies (lesbians) of La Selva introduced a few traditions to the repertoire of activities. One of these was the yearly jumble sale. Only the English lassies really understood the point and fun of this but everyone else joined in with gusto when they realized they could get some good cheap clothes. We all brought what we never wore anymore and hoped to refresh our wardrobes with bargains.

We had a full-scale meeting on the subject. The Catalan ladies oo'd and ah'd as we explained. People in England take their used clothes and stuff to church hall and put everything on tables, to sell very cheaply and earn money for the church. We would get some cash for our bar.

On the day, there were tables piled high with clothes. There was a general hum of conversation and activity and a friendly relaxed atmosphere. There were women grasping beers and rooting through heaps of fabric with spliffs in their mouths, chatting in English, Spanish and Catalan. Soon everyone was in the swing.

"How much is this?"

"50p."

"What?"

"50p."

"You're jokin'."

"No, 50p."

"What a bargain!"

Me and Rosi went along. I reckoned we'd be cool and relaxed there. We could meet friends and be seen out and about together and have a laugh.

As soon as we walked in, I felt Rosa tense up. She drew away from me leaving a gulf of two inches between us. She began to frown. I tried to ignore it and told myself to stop overreacting. We drifted apart and I got into scrabbling through the piles of clothes.

I thought I understood her discomfort and tried to give her space. I made a big effort and tried to chat to her a couple of times, but she was on edge and would turn away from me while I was talking. I felt like everyone's eyes were on us. Rosa didn't seem to care. She didn't even seem to be there.

I went back to the piles of stuff and tried to get involved but my sense of foreboding grew. Finally, I sensed that Rosa had left. I looked around and sure enough, she was gone. I was torn between looking casual and pretending nothing was wrong and going haring after her. I went after her, leaving friends glancing curiously after me.

Rosa was down in the underground, waiting for the next train. She looked at me. Her eyes seemed to plead for understanding.

"Did I do something wrong?"

"Geez what a waste of time," she hissed.

"But I thought we were having fun." She wouldn't look at me.

I was relieved when the train arrived, and we both got on.

I thought she might ask to be left alone but she didn't. She gave me an awkward little hug as we arrived at the top of the five flights of stairs that led to her home. Once inside, she was relaxed, charming and warm and seductive.

I was reeling with the mixed messages. But they filled a yawning gap in my emotional life. I loved talking with Rosa. She was clever and funny. There was a silly little dance that her mother had taught her. Swaying her backside up and down in a figure of eight, looking over her shoulder to check I was watching. And she had some very interesting takes on life. Once I said, "You know Rosa, I'm not going to get old, I don't want to be old." She replied, completely dead pan, "It's better than the alternative."

She listened to me and took me seriously and made me feel beautiful and fascinating. She could listen to me talk about things I'd always kept to myself, for fear of putting people off. Topics like my little brother with his heroin habit were interesting to her. She would sit quite still next to me, listening. She helped me to feel normal.

Women's Day!

It was March 8th International Women's Day and we'd been back together for two months. Rosa had gone to Valladolid. I had asked her to come back for International Women's Day. In the 1990s in Barcelona, this was big news. Women occupied the square where the two main governing bodies, the Catalan and the Spanish, sat facing each other. Each of the government buildings was imposing and beautiful in its own way. Women's bands played all night long on a stage set up in the square. I wanted to be with Rosa and feel the buzz together. She was non-committal. The 8th arrived and I was antsy.

"Holaaa!" she piped down the phone.

"Hullo, how are ya?"

"Fab, having a great time!"

"I'm okay too," I lied, "The atmosphere's great here. There's going to be a band, you know, Juliana and her band of rockers. And a huge party in Pl San Jaume, are you coming back?"

"Don't think so. I'm here with Marc. There're about 10 of us demonstrating outside the town hall here, can you imagine!? We're not going away in a hurry, ha, ha! You have a good time and I'll see ya soon."

"Don't you want to be with me?"

"No, no, no, I'm great here with these girls, thanks."

"Alright, bye, then."

"Byeee!"

I was in a state of turmoil. I wasn't happy for her but felt I should have been. After all, she wasn't doing anything wrong, having a nice time with friends. Maybe, if she had said, "Sorry, Clar, I would have felt more understood. I couldn't see anything clearly."

That evening, I went out alone, feeling numb. I put on some tight jeans and headed to the square. I walked purposefully to Plaza Sant Jaime with a kind of ache behind my eyes. I grinned with relief when Aurora walked up with a smile. She was an old friend I had once slept with. Aurora was small and dark and very sexy, especially since she had a girlfriend and didn't believe in monogamy.

We chatted easily for a while and then with my confidence up, I went off to dance and drink. We bumped into each other later and ended up in my tiny single bed in my rented room. Aurora was so unreservedly joyous about sex that everything seemed okay until later.

The next evening Rosa drove home in her red Renault. I kept checking my mobile for messages and eventually I rang her.

"Hi."

"Hi, where are you?"

"I'm driving through Calatayud."

"Have you seen the new moon."

"Yes, I've got it right overhead, see you soon sweetheart."

"Yes, see you soon, love you."

"Me too."

For the moment, there was nothing wrong. I could explain everything, after all I was right. She had left me high and dry for an important day when she could have come home. She hadn't even told me when she would be back. Hmmmm, no, things weren't quite alright. I wanted her to get back and get it over with.

In bed that night, I told her about my unfaithfulness.

"I was upset when you didn't come back yesterday."

"Yes, but you were okay, weren't you? Did you go out with the girls?"

"Yes."

"Did you dance a lot in Pl San Jaume? I bet Juliana's band was great."

"Yes."

"So, you had a good time?"

"Not really."

"Why not?"

"I wanted to be with you, and I was angry and lonely."

"Why?"

"Because you didn't come back. I missed you."

"Glad you missed me. I missed you too."

"I missed you so much that I slept with Dolores."

"Dolores!"

She turned over and I heard sobbing. She didn't want comforting. She forgave me.

News of affairs travelled fast on the small Barcelona lesbian grapevine. I'd told Katie, and Aurora didn't keep it secret. In fact, she was parading about in white the next day, letting everyone know that something special had happened.

Whenever we saw Aurora from then on, I only said a quick "hello." I felt like everyone was watching me dealing with my guilt. Rosa had never liked her and kept her distance even more. If ever they met, she would greet Aurora politely and talk about the weather. But I could see the muscles in her neck tense up dangerously and knew that I had to keep away.

Plans?

When I first started to date Rosa, I began cautiously, to have visions of a future with her. I imagined her meeting my friends and colleagues and going out together. I thought that Christmas would be different with a lover. I imagined holidays. And in fact, all these things have happened. But none of them were planned with a view to a future. After 18 years of relationship, including a wedding, there was still no ballpark vision for the future. Rosa had her job in the hospital, which she was devoted to, and I had my projects and plans, including a son.

Every time I tried to create a plan for a future, Rosa and I came to blows, literally. I learnt to plot and plan alone and present Rosa with a "fait acomplie." This seemed to upset her less. We could discuss for hours the details of a holiday or pour over web pages of hotels, examining every detail of the rooms. But putting a plan into practice with both of us present, was down to me. I marveled over how Rosa would support my projects without becoming personally involved in them. She would invest her holidays and her wages and even her energy. Still somehow, she remained on the outside.

Our first long trip together, to her university city of Valladolid, was an eye opener. I sensed that we weren't ready to share our intimate past.

She had been to celebrate her birthday there and although she had asked me to go along, I hadn't gone. It felt like we just needed more time alone together before facing friends from the past and family.

My worst-case scenario came true. Rosa couldn't give me any special attention when faced with her ex-girlfriends and friends from her early years. She found it impossible to tear herself away from conversations about past events, people and shared times. The atmosphere of her past absorbed her, and it seemed like she couldn't differentiate it from the present, where I was.

Trailing through the streets of Valladolid behind her and her ex, Ceci, who were all but holding hands and talking avidly, heads close together, I dragged my feet. When Ceci realized that I was feeling bad, she bought me a whiskey and told me to cheer up. Rosa thought she was being sweet.

Finally, sitting on the doorstep of another friend of hers, clutching my knees, I wanted to stop existing. Valentino, Rosa's elegant, architect, gay friend, had a classy studio in one of the centuries old buildings of Valladolid.

"Ceci and Rosa were together a long time, they have a lot of catching up to do," he explained kindly.

I wondered when someone would notice that she had a new girlfriend now. In fact, I wondered when Rosa would remember.

We stayed at another of Rosa's friend's houses. A quaint bungalow built in the 1940s. This was where Rosa had spent most of her youth and she had her own bedroom there. In fact, it had been where she had celebrated her birthday. I felt confused by all the relationships that surrounded Rosa and no one took much trouble to explain them to me. One morning, when I was looking a bit down at breakfast, her friend Vero said, "Why didn't you just let Rosa come on her own, so that she could enjoy being with her old friends."

I reeled at the insult and rejection but explained that Rosa had been there a few months before for her birthday and this time we'd decided to come together. Later Rosa scolded me for not being more cheerful.

I was drowning in Rosa's past, and she wasn't tossing me any lifesaving rings, let alone jumping in to save me herself.

What Now?

I was dizzy with shifts between warm and cold in Rosa. When she was cold, I was heart-broken and didn't have the resources to reason. When she was warm again, I was flooded with relief. All the time in the back of my mind there was a nagging feeling that something strange was going on. I knew she was a lovely woman. But I never, ever felt we were on the same page.

I tried to explain to friends until I was blue in the face, and they were bored with hearing it. The phone calls.

"Oh love, what's happened now?"

"She's gone off again."

"Where to?"

"I don't know, probably to see her brother in Murcia, sob."

I moaned loudly down the phone.

"Hey, hey, hold on I don't think she's gone that far, she usually hangs around a bit and then comes back, doesn't she?"

"Yes," sob, "s'pose so."

"Aww, you wanna come round for a cuppa?"

"No," sniff, "I'd rather be here, thanks."

I didn't want to hang up and be alone again. But what else could I say.

"Thanks, Katie, I, I'll be okay." My voice was flat.

These conversations happened so often that they became my identity. I was the delicate one, the one who needed attention. And I hated myself for it.

I tried to fit my relationship with Rosa into any understanding, I had of loving relationships. This was precious little, and I couldn't. It was all based on the present moment. If there was a conflict, one of us would go off for a while. I learned that if I could go back and pretend that nothing had happened, the good times would come back.

If we stuck it out, there would be a night of anguish after the tiff. We could have hugged and made up. But Rosa was cold and distant and rejected any physical contact. I would push to talk in over. She would stare at the floor or the wall. This could go on for hours. My head spun with ideas to try and bring her out and eventually it was just fury. She had to talk, or I would disappear into nothing.

"Why don't you say something, Rosa?"

"Rosa, can you hear me?"

"Rosa, you see sometimes it helps to talk about things."

Her eyes would begin to close.

"I don't want us to fight. Rosa please, talk to me."

"Rosa, I'm here next to you, I'm a person, why don't you say anything?"

At dawn, I would give up. We would flop exhausted into bed. Rosa would turn over and be snoring in two minutes. I stared at the wall trying not to kick it.

"Rosi, Ro, look at me love. We could talk to a psychologist," I tried, the next day when we were a bit more human.

"What for?" Came the flat question.

"I think we have a problem."

"I have a problem, you don't let me sleep," she snapped nastily from the bathroom where she went every morning for 15 minutes to relieve herself with a Sudoku.

My head spun again, as I held on to my frustration.

I thought, if I could swallow my complaints and ignore the emptiness inside, everything would go back to normal. We were the bright, beautiful, brave lesbian couple. We blazed the trail of single sex happiness again.

We did see a psychologist at a lesbian and gay center. First, we went together.

"Soooo, how are weee?" she eyed us. And I had a vision of her rubbing her hands together and licking her lips. But she was all I had for now.

"Shall I start?" I looked at Rosa and she nodded.

"We have these violent rows where we hit each other."

"Do you talk about it afterward, try to resolve things?"

"No, that's the problem, we never sort anything out. We just separate for a day or two and then start all over again as if nothing had happened."

Rosa was looking out the window.

"Rosa, what do you think of all this?"

She looked confused, as if she didn't know where she was.

"Erm, yeah, yeah, what Clara said. I didn't really want to come."

"Soooo, what do you want out of this, seeing me, I mean." The psychologist looked from one of us to the other.

"I want the rows to finish, and I want to have a peaceful, loving relationship. I love Rosa."

"Hmmm, and you, Rosa."

"Yep, me too!"

We agreed to go separately the next time. The shrink told me to make a list of pros and cons. And she gave me a leaflet on what constituted abuse in a relationship. I thought it a bit rudimentary but did it obediently. Rosa refused to go back after her first visit alone. I squirmed with frustration but realized it was useless to try to persuade her if her heart wasn't in it. Years later, she told me why she hadn't wanted to go back.

Me

Before I started my relationship with Rosa, I had decided to see a therapist. I called her my analyst because it sounded more effective and precise to me than therapist, which smacked of wishy-washy, feel-good to me.

I needed something specific as I had specific problem or three. The one that stood out at the time was an irrational belief that I would "end up with a man," without wanting to. It was terrifying. I knew it was irrational, but it wouldn't leave me alone. I didn't imagine being raped or forced to marry anyone. It was a surreal belief that, somehow, I would be hoodwinked into wanting to be with a man.

My analyst recommended some physical back-up to her sessions and suggested acupuncture. I didn't want to do that because the person she recommended was a man and I didn't want anyone messing with my body. I had messed with it enough myself.

I had spent two years in London, before arriving in Barcelona, working as a full-time barmaid in Leicester Square. I had taken advantage of the time to have sex with as many men as I could fit in and I had got myself pregnant and had an abortion. In my mind, I was looking for love. When I arrived in Barcelona, I had decided to try to find a relationship with a woman. But I had continued to have sex with men. I would drink copiously, and this fitted in well with the ex-pat English teaching scene there.

One evening, I had gone out to drink away the loneliness and frustration of a bad romances with women. I ended up stumbling out of a bar and down to the beach followed by three young Spaniards. There I fucked each one of them in the shallows. They left me there, going off laughing and joking. After this, I knew I needed help.

Instead of an acupuncturist, I saw a psychiatrist that a friend had recommended. This clever woman put me on Synogan, an anti-psychotic drug.

By the time, I had started to see Rosa seriously, I was stable and reducing the dose. Rosa was concerned.

"I know a really good psychiatrist, Clara."

"Do you, now."

"Yeah, you could see her and get a second opinion."

"You what?"

"Y'know get a second opinion, a different perspective."

"My analyst and my psychiatrist are my business, and I am very pleased to be with both of them, thank-you. Anyway, it's none of your business. I shared the information because I trusted you."

"Okay, okay, sorry, it was just a suggestion."

"It's alright, it's just that analysts are very personal, you can't just see anyone."

Sant Joan

The summer equinox in Spain, is called San Joan. People celebrate very noisily with bangers and rockets in Barcelona. It was our first summer together and we were going to throw a party. We cancelled it and recalled it three times on the same afternoon as the party and in the end only a few stragglers turned up. Everyone else had got fed up of holding their breath. I rang my friend Dani for the fourth time.

"Hi Dan!"

"Clara, yes."

"We're having the party after all."

"Well, I think I'm going to Susana's instead, have a nice time." Susana was Dani's girlfriend back then.

I had had high hopes for the get-together. It had seemed like a great idea to get our two sets of friends together. I couldn't look at Rosa and walked out of the flat. I went to La Illa to drink. Later I phoned Rosa.

"Holaaaa, where are you?" Came the cheerful voice.

"In La Illa, drinking." I replied flatly.

"That's nice."

"No, it isn't. Is everyone still there?"

"Well, most of them have gone. It's been great. We went down into the ruins on the old market and saw the tombs."

"Oh, nice."

"Olga is still here but she's on her way out."

"OK well I'll come home then."

"OK see yooo."

Rosa's attic flat looked down on an old market where some archeologists were excavating. We had a bird eye view of it all. It seemed that they'd managed to get into the excavation site and seen some ancient medieval tombs.

Rosa always described her odd little party with affection. She had no idea how disappointed I was that we had been unable to gather our various friends together to get to know each other. It wasn't important to Rosa to have mutual friends.

The next day, Rosa was fine. She didn't notice that I was quiet and withdrawn. I felt odd getting so uptight but couldn't stop thinking about the bad time I'd had. I felt heavy and struggled to get back to a place of fun with Rosa. I knew it was important to do so because I sensed by then that talking things over didn't work. I took all this to my analyst.

Every year, at the beginning of summer, Rosa had a goodbye dinner with her interns. Every year we rowed about it. I tried wheedling, bribing, cajoling and demanding that she not go. It bothered me a lot. There was no rational reason. It was a work do. It was one night a year, and it didn't go on long. It was Rosa's devotion to the occasion. I wanted that same devotion for me. What she gave me wasn't enough. I wanted it all and she didn't have it all to offer me. The dinner symbolized what was missing.

At the beginning, I resorted to drink. I went out and got drunk in the bars of Barcelona alone. The bars of Barcelona are conducive to drinking alone. The old quarter soaked in centuries of human comings and goings with its Medieval streets and courtyards was ideal for losing all sense of time and space. The tiny alleys where no cars fit and the stone churches, take you into a dream world. On corners, you can perch your bottom on the huge worn-out stones. The ones put there, so that the horses and carriages wouldn't break the walls going round corners. There, massive archways lead into the courtyards of ancient palaces, the type of place where Romeo and Juliette would hang out. In those tiny alleys, you could duck into any bar, and you were engulfed in timeless Barcelona.

After quite a few beers, I tearfully rang from my mobile and begged her to come and pick me up. Of course, she would, as soon as she'd finished and where was I, she'd be about an hour, I heard, like from another planet, down the phone. An hour later, I literally tripped out of the bar, falling flat on my face, just as Rosa appeared in the doorway. She regarded me with amusement and a touch of pity. I loathed myself. But I adored Rosa and knew that she had no malice. There was something innocent about the hurt she caused me.

My boundaries were unclear. I didn't have any special things that took priority. I had a teaching job that I did for the money. The only other important being in my life at the time was Stormy. Rosa became my top priority. I went where she led. I was very messy.

Rosa's boundaries were as clear as a limpid mountain pool. She was clear cut. She loved me but she had me in a compartment like the rest of her life.

One summer about four years into the relationship, I ranted while Rosa got dressed. I hated that. I hated getting emotional and I hated her ignoring me. I went onto the big terrace of our attic flat and turned on the hose. I got her attention as I hosed her down inside our living/bedroom. She locked the terrace door on me and carried on and then left. The terrace had a door of wrought iron bars so that we could get the air on hot summer nights without getting robbed.

As I crumpled on the hot terrace floor, I wondered how to get back in. Our downstairs neighbor, Maria had a spare key. Maria was a mother of five who had brought up her family in a flat of 40 square meters with five rooms in total and a tiny balcony.

"Maria, hey, Maria…"

"Clara, is that you?"

"Yes, hey, Maria have you got our spare key?"

"Yes, are you locked out?"

"Yes, could you come up and let me in, please?"

"Sure, hang on a sec."

"Wow, thanks a lot, thought I'd be out there all night."

"Ha, ha, yes, good job I've got spare. Want to keep it for now?"

"Yes, thanks, see you later."

"See yer, Clar."

Aurora's exquisite discretion calmed me a little. Maybe it wasn't such a big deal that I'd hosed down my girlfriend and wet her through and been punished by getting locked out. On one occasion after this, I went with Rosa to one of her work dos. I sat at a huge table in a brightly lit restaurant listening to the life story of someone, I didn't know, because it was her birthday. They had the whole thing on a big screen. The crowd clapped and cheered at pictures of her childhood and adolescence. I sat huddled in a seat next to Rosa's place which was empty. She was with the crowd clapping and cheering. She had tried to introduce me to a couple of strangers who had looked over my shoulder as they said hello. I was right at the same table but felt I was watching from a million miles away. Rosa grinned at me over her shoulder, cheekily inviting me to join in.

Another time, I met with one of her ex's. Rosa was wearing a see-through top with no bra. Her breasts were spectacular.

"Wow! No bra, Rosa? Nice tits, you crazy gal!"

I longed to just laugh along but my face just burned with embarrassment. No one had even looked at me.

Another time at another gathering, the women were in the kitchen. I stuck my face round the door and shyly asked what they were up to.

"Oh nuthin', just mum's stuff."

There was no friendly invitation to join them.

They all had kids and I didn't. I gazed at them for a few seconds and went away again. As soon as Rosa was with a group of friends or colleagues, I ceased to exist for her. I was with people I didn't know and since Rosa ignored me, they mostly, followed her lead.

I stopped trying to share those occasions with her. No matter where we went, I was alone yet surrounded by people, feeling like a piece of snot on a ball gown.

Tinnitus

It's difficult to define what happened when we weren't okay. Fight is not really the word. When we disagreed and it was serious, things just got out of control.

I wanted to talk about how a friend of hers had mistreated me. The conversation was short and to the point.

"Well, you don't have to see her again." She stared at me intensely.

"But I want us to share friends." I spluttered.

"Why? "She continued to stare at me.

"Well…to be able to be more together." I stumbled over the words, all the time with a sinking feeling that they were useless.

"But you're rude to my friends." Once again, her unfailing logic stumped me. She was right.

"They aren't nice to me." I cringed inside and felt like a child trying to explain an awkward predicament to its parents.

"That isn't my fault."

There was no emotion in her voice at this point but as the argument progressed, her face became a screaming, gaping hole with nasty, narrow eyes. After a fight like that, what I should have done was to back down. But I didn't. Or I could watch Rosa storm out. I did that, a lot.

It left me hyperventilating with desperation.

I was restless with Rosa, constantly looking for a change. She was content as long as I didn't get too angry with her or tell her too often that things couldn't go on as they were. I inevitably did this and then she had a meltdown. She would walk out. I would pace and rock and hold my stomach. My guts turned and writhed inside, and my head spun with alternative lives without Rosa. I cried and wailed, and Storm snuggled up to me. I rang a friend knowing everything was hopeless.

"She's gone again." I sobbed down the phone.

"You know she'll come back she always does."

"But I don't know where she is."

"She won't have gone so far. You know that Clar. She's probably parked up somewhere cooling down."

"But I feel panicky."

"Do what you would do to comfort a friend, do that for yourself."

I hung up reluctantly, knowing there was no more to be said. Then I got in my old VW Golf and raced to a car park where she had spent a night once before. It was the Health Centre car park, near our house. It was empty at night and a good place for Rosa to chill after a meltdown. While I had imagined her miles away, she had been two minutes down the road.

She wasn't there and my head just exploded, and a tinnitus began in my ears that never went away. Later, when the fight had blown over, Rosa took me to her hospital to get it diagnosed. I was told there wasn't a cure for tinnitus.

Other times, I'd phone her repeatedly until she screamed down the phone at me. According to her irate shrieks, I was the beginning and end of all her woes. She wanted to see me dead. Then I'd shift from desperation to fury and match her, and some. The Post Traumatic Shock Syndrome became quite common for me.

Once after a fight, I had gone to a friend's house. Katie was having party and we had been invited. Only I went due to the fight.

With my gut in a knot, I kidded myself that maybe Rosa had calmed down. I longed for her to be there. I rang.

Rosa's voice spat at me over the phone, "You fucking bitch, do you know where I am? I'm at Bellvitge hospital. They're testing me for a heart tremor. You've nearly killed me this time. You want me dead, don't you?"

I had heard this kind of talk before and was more sad than shocked. I didn't rush to hospital because I thought that if she was irate with me, my being there would only make her worse. I didn't realize that her fury was like a cry for help.

"No, I wanted to ask how you were and whether you wanted to come to Katie's. I miss you."

"Miss me? You don't bloody miss me, you smother me. Since you've been around, I've seen none of my friends, my family might as well not exist, I can't go to hospital dos without you soaking me first and now you say you miss me!"

"Please, Rosa, I love you and want to be with you."

"You don't know what love is…"

Rosa ranted for a little longer and then cut off.

Once again, I was all alone. Katie looked at me, head tipped to one side.

"Still cross with you?" She asked looking me in the eye with a little frown.

Cross, such a gentle little word. I clung to its normality.

Later I crept home, my heart feeling very low. When I arrived, Rosa was calm and cool. I knew I had to pretend that we could get back to normal without talking. If I tried to talk, the same outbursts would happen again.

These more frequent outbreaks were like water on a stone. Gradually they wore away my surface.

I found that if I could pretend that nothing had happened, then I could enjoy the part of being with Rosa that was like magic. The adventures, the sex and the company could maybe be enough to buffer the fights.

Fury

It became evident very early on, that both Rosa and I both had fiery tempers. In the kitchen part of her apartment, we argued. I was getting anxious over something.

"Rosa, listen to me, I need to talk about this."

She regarded me sidelong with a packet of flags in her hand. She looked scornful and began to get a cigarette out.

"Don't ignore me Rosa, this is important to me."

She continued preparing to smoke.

"I'll have one too then." I felt desperate to find common ground. I didn't usually smoke.

"No, you won't, they're mine."

"Oh, come on…you've got a whole packet."

"Yes, and they're mine."

"Gimme one…"

We found ourselves on her kitchen floor, scrapping like school kids. I wasn't scared of the kicks, and they didn't hurt, physically. The physical violence was just a symptom of frustration on both parts. On the surface of it, the fight was over a packet of fags, or at least that's how Rosa remembers it. For me, however, it was something more emotional. I don't know how it began but I do remember a desperate feeling of abandonment, which was beginning to surface with Rosa. The cigarettes were just a way of getting her attention. They seemed more important to her, than what I was trying to express and so became the subject of the tussle. I took her incapacity to give me attention as unwillingness.

In the end, I left her flat to go home, feeling sad and angry but unable to shake off my attachment to her. There were various other occasions on which we fought physically and gave each other bruises. Friends were discrete and didn't ask.

It's strange, how violence between a man and a woman, shocks so much more and is more visible than violence between two women or an adult and children. Between two women in our case in was accepted and absorbed into the community.

On another occasion, my fingers were slammed in a door by accident and one of them broke. It was a time when Rosa had invited neighbors to come up to her attic flat, which I now inhabited full time, to fix an aerial on the roof. She hadn't mentioned this to me, and the technician caught me unawares, of course. When Rosa got home, I wanted an apology or some kind of recognition that she had not been quite nice to me and when there was none, I became irate. As usual we both hit 10 on the Richter scale in record time and Rosa is a fight or flighter so being a basically decent person she flew. I tried to stop her and she slammed the door.

Immediately, it was obvious that something not good had happened to my finger, so Rosa called Peter the very neighbor invited to fix his arial, to take us to the nearest hospital. I marveled at her practicality, quick thinking and cool head. No questions were asked, and my finger was fixed up. Rosa was very concerned about my finger but not my emotions and was, in fact, still very angry with me for causing such a fuss.

Later, when I had to go about with my finger splinted and told the truth about what had happened, she got cross about me flaunting. I didn't mean to flaunt but it did seem dangerous to start hiding our violence.

Staying at a friend's place while we renovated our newly purchased attic flat, we had another bad row. It was one evening at about bedtime. I can't remember exactly why; it was usually something emotional of mine clashing with Rosa's inability to manage emotions at all. I never let things go and insisted up to breaking point. I do remember trying to take her joint from her. I wanted her to pay me more attention than her joint. This time, Rosa punched me one in the face and broke one of my small front teeth. She was beside herself with desperation and anger at me for provoking her and with herself for lashing out. She always admitted to having a violent side but said that I was the only one who brought it out in her.

I don't blame her and indeed feel little anger for these outbursts of ours, I left Rosa with bruises too sometimes and she forgave quickly, but I felt the situation could get out of control, so I began to look for help. Rosa didn't need help. For her, once the moment was past, it was not only forgotten but lost and any attempt at discussion just recreated the same situation instead of allowing for progress.

Rosa felt either love or hate and each moment was the only truth. At least that is how it seemed to me. I suffered so many changes from warm to cold and so quick, in Rosa, that I was reeling, trying to keep up with her mood changes. I couldn't believe it when she turned on me and after a time, I couldn't believe when she was nice to me either, I was always expecting the worst and when the worst happened, I couldn't believe it. There was never a moment of complete togetherness between us. I would try to explain this to friends. They talked about symbiotic lesbian relationships and carefully explained that I had, in effect, to get a life. It seemed that if I could just get enough outside interests, things would go better, in other words I would feel better. Rosa was oblivious to my distress, except when I became bothersome, and she had a meltdown.

This all fell in with my own deep feelings about myself. I was needy and problematic and struggling to be independent.

I began a Masters in Women's Studies at Barcelona University, which helped assuage the constant emptiness. The master's was fascinating and took two years and, in that time, I made new friends.

Lonely

About four years into our relationship, I began to suffer very badly from asthma. The pollution in the center of Barcelona was getting worse. We couldn't talk about the problem. This was normal by now. So, we would look for temporary solutions. One of these, one Christmas, was a friend, Maite's chalet, in the pretty little Pre Pyreneen village of Olot. The frost covered the ground and forest trees with a sparkly, white veil and when it snowed everything was quiet and created a feeling of awesome reverence.

Driving along the icy mountain track, craning our necks to make out the precipitous edge, we laughed and joked together. Storm the cat sat at the windscreen staring out into the mist. I was keen to get there and egged Rosa on. She was more cautious and had her doubts about arriving at all.

Suddenly a yellow Raleigh car appeared out of the mist. Then another surreal apparition trundled round a bend and another. A little further on, one of them was stuck, teetering riskily over edge of the track. We stopped to talk to the driver. He was waiting for help. Soon a snow plough heaved into sight, and we knew we were nearly somewhere.

Rosa and I were planning to spend a night together. Then she would go down to Barcelona for work until Christmas Eve. I would spend three nights there, with Stormy, until Rosa joined me. I was fine with the idea and feeling proud of myself for not getting all insecure and abandoned. I was learning to be alone within my relationship. This is what I told myself. It felt like I was making progress. We had our romantic night and then Rosa went back to work.

Everything seemed other-worldly. The place only had one bar and the shop was open at the weekends, for tourists. The narrow, cobbled streets were mostly empty. Old stone cottages all inhabited by someone, puffed wood smoke out of squat chimneys, the only sign of their mysterious occupants.

Fresh, chilly air stung my nose as I stepped gingerly on icy cobble stones. A few winter birds chirped, and I could hear every tiny gust of wind that whispered through the deserted streets. Sometimes, a cloud came to cover the buildings in it's misty cloak. And a watery sun, illuminated the surrounding hills with an eerie glow. A red sun sank early behind those hills in the evening.

Brief glimpses of people on my ambles round the village, were disconcerting as I wandered around in a dream.

My imagination began to work. I began writing a book. It was pure fantasy about all animals in the village. With my cat Storm as the main character, working as witches and warlocks in cahoots with African animals, they confront evil. They seemed to come to life, and I was happy to be alone thinking that Rosa was out there caring and would soon be back with me. I even enjoyed the solitude for a while.

I found myself easily distracted and noticed every noise and every cloud that passed. I explored the kitchen in detail and cooked with the few ingredients I had. I sat on the tiny balcony with Stormy staring out at the other houses and squinting to see signs of life while pretending to write my book.

A little Siamese kitty took up with us and occupied one of the bedrooms. I worried that Maite would not approve and felt I was betraying her generosity. I let the cat stay anyway. Storm tolerated her as long as she didn't come to close to the wood burner.

I spent the time exploring the surrounding hills while Storm waited for me. The expeditions for collecting firewood kept me occupied too. It was like a retreat without the total peace of mind. In fact, despite the silence and the idyllic surroundings, I couldn't really relax.

Walking through the shadowy pine and Holme oak woods, was a relief. The sharp dry air cleared the cobwebs after damp, polluted Barcelona. I took off my jacket, walking briskly and pushing through the undergrowth, working up a sweat. The woods were spookily quiet; no birds or other signs of life. I knew that somewhere in the undergrowth there were wild pigs minding their own business. I kept my mind occupied making up stories about mysterious half ruined houses and a lone hunting dog that I spotted and who spotted me in the distance. We looked at each other for some time and I fantasized about it passing on a secret message.

Finally, the solitude got the better of me and I wanted to share things with Rosa. I knew that if I phoned, her tone would be cold and unresponsive, so I phoned my analyst. It took the edge off the loneliness.

On the second day, I rang Rosa for our daily chat.

"How's it going?"

"Good, good. I think I'm going to stay for the Christmas do."

"What? Why? I don't want you to."

"The weather is foul and I don't think, I'll be able to set off on Christmas Eve."

"But you promised."

"Yes but I've changed my mind."

"Oh."

"Have you got enough food and firewood?"

"Yes, yes, I go out collecting firewood every day, it's part of the fun, that's not the problem but it's pretty lonely."

"Well, I'll see you on Christmas day, Bye."

Conversations over the phone were always strangely emotionless and often left me emptied out.

My hands trembled as I hung up. Twenty-four more hours to wait represented much more than one day. They represented someone who preferred to be with the work crowd, to with me. I didn't really believe the bit about the weather. We had made it up practically through a snowstorm.

I paced the apartment looking in every room for some kind of distraction, asking Stormy why Rosa couldn't understand. Finally, I flopped down on the bed, and cried.

I rang my stepfather in Hong Kong, the only surefire nerve calmer. He comforted me and prepared me to hang on another night.

I'd fallen in love with my stepfather Rusty, before he married my mum. I was 15 and he was 31 with long tennis legs and a relaxed inviting manner. He had played tennis in Malawi where they had lived, and he had won championships. He had been a professor at the University of Zomba and hob nobbed with the vice president of the country and had a white Ford Capri. He gave me Sobrani Black Russian cigarettes and introduced me to Bacardi and lime. We did a road trip from Malawi to Kenya together with my little brother, who was eight and by the end I was hopelessly in love.

By the time I was with Rosa, we were laughing buddies and he lived in Hong Kong.

"Hullo! Clara!"

"Yes, it's me what time is it there?"

"About 2 am."

"Oh shit, I'm sorry!"

"No, Noooo…carry on, I wasn't sleeping anyway."

"Well…" and I told my story.

"Well don't let her know how upset you are. Is it good for walking?"

"Yes, it's gorgeous."

"Well, there you are, a good long walk cures nearly everything."

"Ha, ha, ha."

"Ha, ha, well you know… so, do you think she's being unfaithful?"

"Nooooo!"

"So…what's the problem? Go back to bed and get a good night's sleep and go for a really, long walk tomorrow."

I managed to laugh and went back to bed. My thoughts were a jumble. Really nothing was very wrong, but I couldn't rest. Storm purred noisily into my ear to drown out the cacophony of negative thoughts.

The day Rosa arrived, I was determined to be in a good mood and planned to go for a long walk and be sure to find her waiting for me when I got back.

It was a bright, frosty Christmas morning. I only had a vague idea of where I was heading, following a path without a map I left the village behind. I walked through some low pastures with cows grazing on the edges of the forest. Further on, a stone cottage appeared out of the blue and some cats sat there staring at me. There was no fence to show that it was a private property. A woman came out of the house, and we said hello. She lived there and invited me in. There was no electricity or running water but there was a sense of peace and contentment about her.

We said goodbye and I carried on along the path which wound into the forest and crossed a stream and then started to climb a steep hill. Sometimes I climbed over a style or stopped to turn and see how far I'd climbed. I was very aware of being alone as I stopped to stare at lichen covered rocks and tiny flowers.

Eventually, I arrived at a high up prairie and stopped there to eat a sandwich. The scrubby, grey green grass covered the tough, stony ground and it scratched my legs as I sat down. The absolute silence was eerie and closed in on me until I decided to turn for home.

Nearing the village, I pushed my hands deep in my pockets and told myself not to expect anything. I'd been gone all day, but a little voice told me that Rosa wouldn't be there.

She wasn't there but Stormy came running to the door purring. I cried and went to the kitchen to prepare some supper. Finally, around 5 pm, Rosa turned up. She was radiant and laden with food for Christmas. But Christmas was over for me. I'd spent the day alone and resentful. When she saw the state I was in, she was more angry than sympathetic. Her eyes narrowed and she told me about the bad roads and how she hadn't been able to set off in the morning. We spent the next two days circling each other like two lionesses until I was exhausted and gave up the fight. Christmas in Spain is not the same as in England. There is not such a big build up now so much emphasis on Christmas day.

On Hold

I usually suggested having sex. But Rosa was always happy with that. I complained sometimes about being the one to ask. She didn't see a problem. I stopped worrying about it.

I discovered that we could have pleasant and caring sex, regardless of how the rest of our relationship was going. We loved each other's bodies and when we had sex, I always blocked our problems out of my mind. There was enough worthwhile in our relationship, for me to be able to make love. Rosa seemed able to compartmentalize the occasion and put a parenthesis on our spats, in order to offer herself a spot of relief. the way I did it, was to convince myself that things were going to change, and we were going to do other things better too. Rosa seemed content with the moment in itself, and it had no further consequences as far as she was concerned. But I was wary when things were not happy between us. I would have an aftermath, a bit like an emotional hangover. I would build up hopes just to realize, that nothing changed.

This was exhausting and our sex life suffered. We could, according to Rosa have sex as often as we made up. But I began to feel more and more reluctant to open myself up and put myself in the vulnerable mood I needed, to make love.

I put sex on hold. In the same way as I would initiate sex, I put a conscious end to it. We still cared. But because there was never any progress made, I had to begin an end, somewhere. I think that for Rosa, it was just business as usual without the sex.

I had tried to discuss the evolution of our relationship as I saw it, with Rosa, just to see if we were, at least, on the same page. I wanted to know if she was happy to carry on as we were. After about 15 minutes of my own monologue, I would begin to doubt my own reasons and give up. The only meaningful concession I could make toward voicing my doubts, was to stop having sex with Rosa.

Rosa never remembered that it was always me who had initiated the sexual encounters, she just knew, she missed them.

She treated the whole situation as if it didn't exist. I think now, that for her it really didn't exist. The situation that I refer to is the fact that I needed change to happen for the relationship to carry on.

To me, it was as clear as day that if I woke up every night that we slept in the same house, and wept at about three in the morning, there was something not working for us. I had my hormones checked, as Rosa and others suggested, and everything was okay in that department. I was willing to admit that Ben, my little boy, drove me crackers sometimes but the state of exasperated desperation and hopelessness that I got into were not to do with Ben.

We could have taken off where we had left off any day. The attraction was still very much alive. The rows and screams and shouts and the interrupted nights, in which the only solution to avoid nearly killing each other was for one of us to walk out at two in the morning, were not good reason to re-examine our sexual relationship, for Rosa. They were for me.

There was still a strong attraction after 17 years of being together, no problems there. If I could have had some guarantee that the changes I needed, would have happened, I would have welcomed Rosa back into my bed. But there was never any guarantee.

Little by little I killed that side of my love for Rosa, for the sake of survival.

Release

Lie-downs happened when I had to lie down in the street to cope with my tangled emotions.

After signing the contract to buy our little attic flat, I tried to understand what had happened in the big conference room, where we'd signed, in the presence of lawyers and the vendor. I had no idea of Spanish law, regarding buying and selling houses and the jargon was over my head. I tried asking Rosa to explain. This was a mistake. Rosa can explain perfectly and clearly the process for a complicated brain surgery, so that I can understand it. But if I asked her to explain something pertaining to everyday life, we were capable of whipping up quite a storm together.

We ended up running down a main street of Barcelona screaming at each other. A lie down was the next stage.

Years later, we were in the middle of the old quarter of Barcelona once, arguing about whether to leave that flat in the center or not. Rosa's reasoning was impeccably logical. If I wanted to leave because of my asthma, then she couldn't stop me. She was adamant and completely fair. It didn't occur to her that I might not want to leave but needed to for my health and quality of life. Nor did it occur to her to make the sacrifice of coming with me. She couldn't imagine how it would be living without me, so it didn't bother her, the idea of leaving the place where she lived bothered her more.

I was left with a rubbish dump of useless emotions. Looking around to check there was no one else there, I lay down, on the ancient paving stones of Plaza del Joanet, where we had ended up and gazed at the plane trees and pigeons. I hoped they wouldn't shit on me. I admired the old drinking fountain from the ground. Rosa regarded me with pursed lips, shifting from one foot to the other and looking around nervously. Then she stormed off. After a while I picked myself up, feeling a bit more at home with absurdity. Then the ache of loneliness began to crawl into my stomach, heart and finally my brain.

There was another similar incident associated with leaving our flat and my sense of abandonment. We had by then moved out of the flat but were still paying the mortgage, as well as another rent. The argument was about whether to rent out the flat or not. Rosa got her little back pack and walked out.

"Go on then, bugger off!" I screamed after her.

Once she'd gone, that awful loneliness crept in. About ten minutes later, I went after her in the car and caught up just as she turned into a country track, leading into town. I got out of the car and called to her and went running after her but she carried on. She wanted to quietly meltdown and then, compose herself. I wasn't having any of that and knowing that the one thing that would get her attention was me catching cold; I lay down in a big muddy puddle at my feet. It had been raining heavily. I mused about Peppa Pig and it occurred to me that I had only once before sat in a puddle in Cyprus after a very long dry season. It got Rosa on the move. She was with me in seconds, and we went home together in the car. She was very concerned about me catching cold and still very angry. I pretended to be worried about catching cold too. It drew attention away from the real issue and I was learning that, that worked well.

I was beginning to learn what bothered Rosa and to use it to get her to take notice of me. The basic arguments and problems never changed, but I was getting her attention.

A bothersome little grain of shame scratched at my brain. But I formed a protective cover around it like an oyster. Pity the result wasn't a pearl.

Eventually, about six years later, Rosa came to the conclusion that the quality of life is better outside the city. She had had to find out for herself and not from me. She eventually followed me out of the city, into a pretty little apartment not too far away for her to commute, and agreed to rent out our apartment.

Friends

A pattern began to emerge regarding our friends. Whenever I got close to anyone, Rosa found some fault in the person's character and harangued me and treated my friend so badly that in the end, I give up on the relationship. She found it easy to find fault in people who, either she hadn't known for years, or were not connected to work or some other institute she identified with.

It had started with my best friend, Katie. I consulted her about everything, affairs of the heart and soul. She was in there at the beginning of my adventure with Rosa. Like a true friend, she had wanted to know all the juicy details. I so wanted her and Rosa to like each other. But Rosa took almost instant exception to her. I didn't know the reason. But, I remember comments about not being able to take her to the mountains to ski because she was fat and might break Rosa's old Renault Express. Katie soon picked up on Rosa's hostility and began to give us, as a couple, a wide berth. This made me feel all the more vulnerable to the dismissive treatment that I got from Rosa's group of friends. "Friends" very quickly became an issue.

I liked a young woman called Aranxa, on the master's course; she was irreverent, daring and fresh. She was a friend; I was totally in love with Rosa but liked to have close friends. Rosa noticed there was something special about Aranxa and began a campaign to keep her away from me. Aranxa had a dodgy Moroccan boyfriend who gave a lot of trouble in the end. For Rosa, this was a very good reason not to trust her. We had heated rows over her before I established a distance. I gave up the struggle of sentiment over logic and the friendship died a death. Aranxa and I became acquaintances.

I discovered that I could have as many groups of friends as I wished. I could stay away without checking in as much as I liked, she didn't worry or fret as I would. The problems began, if I made a special friend. That was unbearable for her.

Personally I don't like group friendships, they make me twitch. I get paranoid when I think that what I've said to one person, is floating around in the ether for anyone to catch. Rosa loved groups and networks and big get-togethers, it was how she operated.

She kept all her buddies from university days and would see them once a year. They were scattered around the country and travelled miles to see each other for a dinner.

Rosa enjoyed exchanging pleasantries with neighbors and was always very well up, on what was going on in our street. She was also very well liked. She is a likeable person.

She was loyal and generous and didn't ask much in emotional terms for her friendship. She valued favors very highly and always remembered to pay them back. One of her frequent phrases on the phone used to be, "Call anytime you like, I'll be here and do anything I can to help."

I would feel the muscles in the back on my neck tense up and my heart quickened as I imagined all kinds of invasions to my privacy. In fact, no one did ever ring in the middle of the night.

Little by little the tension and stress of all these small irritations began to get the better of my body and my asthma got bad.

She was happy just to see work colleagues at work and in fact, people I labelled as her work colleagues were her closest friends. There were not many of them but she was happy with them and valued them highly.

Rosa also maintained good relationships with her ex's although, again, she saw them rarely She counted them amongst her best friends. She never invited a friend home just to have a cupper and a chat.

My relationships with her friends, weren't good. There were only a few who liked me and I tolerated precious few of them. Every now and then, we would make a list of the ones I managed not to actively hate. I felt like none of them saw me as a person, but as a rather irritating appendage.

After 18 years of relationship, there were less than a handful that didn't exactly leap with joy on seeing me, but hadn't openly offended me.

Looking back, I think some of them tried to welcome me, but I was unreceptive, and they were not inclined to try very hard.

Issues

Sleep became an issue very early on. Again, here there was the mixture of delight and nightmare that kept me stimulated.

I slept in Rosa's flat quite a lot and sometimes she would share my little bed in my minute single bedroom. I was a light sleeper and have had insomnia. I didn't consider it to be a problem when I met Rosa. I had got over it. I needed a relaxed atmosphere and wind down time before bed, though. If we both went to bed together and fell asleep at the same time, it was delicious.

I remember one night early on when Rosa had gone out for a drink with a friend. I stretched out in the double bed looking forward to Rosa slipping in beside me later. I was in a warm, cozy, slumber when Rosa arrived back. She banged the door shut, switched on the big, top light and started to get ready for bed. I couldn't understand what I'd done to make her angry. Then I got angry and thought she was drunk. She was surprised. She told me that she'd had a lovely time and had no idea that she was bothering me. I couldn't believe that she wasn't trying to get my back up. That was the first time I remember sleep being an issue between us.

Rosa normally had a gift for dropping off to sleep wherever and whenever there was an opportunity. As she was an anesthetist in a big general hospital, she'd learned to cat nap, very efficiently. Doctors in Spain have to do that. At least twice a week, there were 24-hour shifts during which, doctors had to be present in the hospital, not just on call. Apart from that, she is a deep sleeper. She enjoys drifting off in front of the telly.

I hate drifting off, or not, in front of the telly. Nights facing the wall to block out the light of the machine, wearing earplugs and eye masks, eventually got up my nose. We couldn't talk about it without coming to blows.

Years Gone By

Wildly different sensations swept through me with Rosa. One minute I was in love and admiring her way of being in the world. The next I couldn't stand her. The make or break came months later, when we were fighting a lot and she had had numerous meltdowns during which I either sent her away or she ran off. I had crazy moments too; howling, weeping, throwing things and behaving very badly, especially considering I had a three-year-old son. He seemed to weather everything very well, as long as I tried to explain what was happening. That would be another story on parenting.

It seemed that at some point Rosa made the decision that she was "in" for the family. She wanted her family and she would do anything within her power to preserve that. I say, "within her power," because not everything was within her power. She couldn't understand me or empathize. She could promise to go a visit an expert on Asperger's Syndrome, but she still couldn't really see why. She didn't need fixing she was fine in herself.

The magical thing was, as far as I was concerned, that she was there for me, as much as she had ever been. This didn't solve my problem of (seeming) lack of affection and empathy, but it did mean that I had a rock. What was better? To split up with someone and break down and have to build yourself up materially and emotionally again, or to be in a kind of limbo where you can't actually split up because one of you simply doesn't see that as an option. I had feelings for Rosa so it was complicated. But as the months went by my, feelings shifted from utter panic of abandonment, when she buggered off during her meltdowns, to frustration and confusion.

Which was better? For me, personally, the frustration and confusion, because it was more to do with the present. My panic at being abandoned came from my ancient history and it was partly what had kept me with Rosa long enough to get to know her as well as I did.

If she was in meltdown and it concerned me, then, according to her, I was the very devil.

"What! You say you love me. You don't know what love is, you're just like your mum a nasty little manipulator. And you sit on our arse all day waiting for me to come home and give you kisses and spend all my bloody money on your little projects. I can't even go and see my friends in Valladolid in peace without you ringing up and moaning to me. In fact, I don't have any friends left because of you, and my family don't want to know me now. Can't you see the mess you're making of everything and as for this stupid business about psychologists… We don't need a psychologist, we need a divorce and I would divorce you if I thought you'd leave me alone once and for all."

She would carry on. At first, I would try to interrupt and plead and beg her to listen. I wept and reasoned. Eventually

I would just hold the telephone away from my ear or scream back at her.

"Shut up, shut up, just bloody shut up! If you divorce me, I'll torment you for the rest of your life."

This was the gist of it. The exact words, I can't recall. When the meltdown passed, she didn't know why I was so bothered about what she had said to me. She had been angry. Neither was she concerned about what I'd said to her, or so it seemed.

During the meltdown, she couldn't remember what she saw in me. My mind twirled in a dervish dance of reasoning and madness. The old saying, "You can't unsay what's said," in Rosa's case was not true. For Rosa, things were not just unsaid but they were not even anywhere anymore. I held it all inside, the good and the bad. I felt like I'd lost my foothold on reality. I was on shifting ground. Someone made me feel important and needed sometimes and at other times she seemed to hate me. Love and hate are part of the same thing, I told myself. One thing was for sure, I was the center of attention.

Slowly, I began to work out a pattern and style of how Rosa's mind worked and to notice how I functioned too. I used to attach emotion to everything said and done. With Rosa, this was a mistake. She very rarely had bad intentions and often her intentions weren't as good as I thought. Rosa acted from her own perspective. She was a lovely person. But she didn't do things for me.

What I had to do is find a way to laugh at her Aspie magic instead of taking it so much to heart and letting it hurt. If I had stayed with her, it would have been my destruction instead of my joy. And there was joy to be had.

I still remember "the good times." It was easier from a distance to accept Rosa as she was and to love her like that.

It was a kind of magic that I felt so cross and wanted to hurt her and prove that I could go it alone and she just used to say, "Well I'll sleep in the flat tonight, Ana's moved out and it's free, would you like me to collect Ben from school or should I stay away?" We had a flat in the center of Barcelona. What more could I say? "Shit, fuck, bugger, bum, piss, cock, fart," but it all disappeared into the ether.

Brother

My brother has a heroin habit that was not going to go away. He's 55 now and started gently easing himself into drugs at about 16, with marihuana in Malawi. He would roam the town where my family lived, and it was no problem to get hold of some really good stuff. By the time he was 18 and finishing secondary school in Hong Kong (the family had moved again), he'd tasted heroin. And he never looked back.

The fact is, that by the time we were in our thirties, my brother and I were estranged. We had no quarrel; we were a splintered family and never saw each other. When I talked with Rosa about all this, she became quite concerned. She had evidently taken quite a lot of notice that night, some years ago, on the steps of an old church in Barcelona, one Autumn evening, when I'd rambled on about my family. She wanted me to see John.

We set off in the Summer of 2001, in her new Peugeot Partner. We crossed France on the way to England, to look for my brother and meet my aunty Ann. The trip is a story in itself, full of Aspie-isms good and bad but the general idea was to go in search of my brother. Pilar and I were always better when we had a common cause. Crusading against a bigger, badder world out there, brought us together. And I was kind of thankful that Pilar had awoken the dormant love that I felt for my 'black sheep' brother.

As we got nearer to where my brother stayed, in a small seaside town in south-west England, communication proved more and more difficult. John lived in protected accommodation. He needed protecting from himself and drug dealers. Rosa began to suspect foul play. My mother was the go-between for us to find John. Whenever we tried to ring her, her phone was either off or had no cover. The only time we spoke to her, she casually told us, she'd taken John up north to visit some friends of hers. My mum knew I had intended to try and find John during my visit to the UK, I'd let her know by internet and told her, more or less, when we'd be able to see him. She knew how difficult it was to catch him in. Rosa was very suspicious that my mum was making it hard for me. I didn't believe it. I just thought she was dilly, absent minded about it. Since then experience has proven Rosa right. It was an example of her incisive mind, un-fogged by emotion.

In the end, we returned to Spain, not having been able to track down John and having had a huge row.

Later that year, in the Winter Rosa suggested that we catch a flight straight to Southampton airport and hire a car to go and find John. She advised me not to tell my mum. We found John and he was delighted to see us.

There was a tiny harbor where private boats moored. We went out for an evening meal and then John led us to a shadowy part of the harbor to smoke a joint with Rosa. We huddled together, stamping our feet and rubbing our hands together, watching our breath on the air. Rosa and John shared a joint. My heart warmed a little as I watched them. I had often wished that time with John would go quicker. I would focus on cleaning his pad and doing a shop. This time, I relaxed a bit.

The next day we went and had fish and chips for lunch. Memorable for being the best fish and chips I'd had and Rosa's first. And, because it was a good time with John. We sat in the back street café grinning a lot and feeling connected.

Rosa and John got on well. They had the subject of drugs, both medicinal and recreational in common. Rosa was non-judgmental. John had done a bachelor's degree in marine biology and knew his science. He was also highly intelligent and took his drug addiction seriously. He had researched all the ins and outs of the various medical drug alternatives. Rosa, an anesthetist and hash enthusiast, also knew all about drugs. She was a great ally and asset for me on that trip and had a lot of impartial insight into John's way of being. At first, I found this hard to swallow but learnt that it helped rather than hindered the relationship between John and me. We found we could only be with John a short time and always at the risk him taking us off on a goose chase, looking for a fix.

One foggy winter's night in England, on another trip to see John, we set off with him to meet one of his "chums."

"This won't take long. Just hang about in the car park until I'm out."

We both knew what was going on. Pointless to say anything, it was. On the way to the rendezvous, Rosa drove straight across a mini roundabout through the thick mist. Rosa is an excellent driver and can pick up any car in any country and have it on the road in five minutes. Driving over a roundabout in England spoke volumes about her deep feelings for John and his problem.

I don't think I could have re-established contact with my brother without Rosa's help – and she knew it. After that first trip, I made a point of meeting him once a year.

My brother has been one of the few people with whom I've talked about Asperger's Syndrome, who hasn't left me feeling like a fool afterwards. I say a fool, meaning that I shouldn't have talked. Not that I'm mistaken about Asperger's. He just listened.

Preps

We were to go up to Norway from Barcelona in Rosa's new Peugeot Partner and we were both enthusiastic about the idea. Some of the best parts of a holiday are in the preparation, especially a road trip. We had to get the car ready and plan the food and the route.

I was hurt when I discovered that Rosa had already decided to prepare the car with an old friend of hers, who was visiting Barcelona. Apparently, Silvi had experience in these things. She'd prepared her own van and knew how. We had a row and Rosa took my disappointment as jealousy. I didn't understand that for her, efficiency and effectiveness were more important than the feeling of sharing. She didn't understand that for me, sharing responsibilities would help cement our relationship and make me feel secure. I didn't care if the bed in the van wasn't perfect.

I felt betrayed and couldn't get beyond preparing the van. I felt a bit sick and didn't want to use a bed someone else had prepared. This someone was another who'd been rude to me, so there was no friendship there. Silvi had come round to what was now our home, while we were out. I had arrived, looking forward to relaxing and maybe, preparing something to eat for myself and Silvi. I still wanted to make peace with her. As I walked in, she turned to me from the studio kitchen and with a sullen twist on her face said.

"I've made a courgette omelet, want some?" She didn't sound friendly, and she didn't smile I got the impression she thought I was intruding.

My heart sank. I felt the unwelcome anger igniting inside me, again. I so wanted to be cool and friendly. Already sore about the preparation of the van, this was too much for me. She had invaded my space as well as my holiday. I swallowed the rage inside but didn't share Silvi's omelet. How much pain for nothing and how much confusion? In hindsight I think we were both overreacting as a result of Rosa's unclear messages.

I had looked forward to doing this with Rosa and lost a bit of the spark of enthusiasm for the trip.

As time went by I found that Rosa would rely on old friends, work colleagues or other tried and tested people, rather than let us work things out together. This left a gaping hole in our relationship as far as I was concerned and there were a lot of rows about it.

It seems she was looking back to her past for sustenance, to her old friends and I was relying heavily on her for a future.

Norway

The trip to Norway, in Rosa's new Peugeot van, was eventful.

We motored through France and up to Switzerland where I remember a magical crazy night, beside some Swiss lake. As we drew near to the lakeside, to park for the night, Rosa drove the van over a huge log and got stuck.

"Oh shit," she muttered revving the engine.

"Uh oh! Let me get out and see," I offered.

Somehow, we struggled free.

Then, I smoked a large joint and waded into to lake fully dressed as Rosa giggled hysterically. I think she had smoked the joint too. Smoky was with us on the trip. She watched us knowingly.

We had to call in at a Peugeot garage the next day to check out the damage under the van. The damage was slight but our argument, as Rosa ignored me when I asked her to explain (I don't know much about cars), was not.

We continued on through Germany, where we had another row and ended up sleeping in a filthy, rat-infested car park, instead of a cute riverside campsite. I spent the night downing wine, wandering around the car park and wailing. The argument this time was about whether to park in the campsite next to some very close neighbors or to leave and find another place. Rosa won. Rosa developed vertigo that night.

We soldiered on through Denmark, where we began to thaw. And finally, we arrived in Norway.

On that trip, I swam in freezing fjords and we camped in deserted spots. Peace came sometimes and unity. Preparing food and eating and laughing about Smoky, who took most everything in her stride, brought us together. We made a good team, the three of us. Rosa, the driver and me the map reader we thought we didn't need anyone else.

Smoky, meeting a strange Norwegian animal as it peeped out of its hole on a wild hillside, had us smiling. And when she missed her footing and fell into a stream and had to swim, saved us from a brewing fight.

I remember the trip with affection as well as sadness. It was amazing that we took our Smoky all that way. It was amazing that we got that far. We shared the wonder of the fjords and winding mountain roads and wild woods. We shared the desire for adventure.

Twists and Turns

Our relationship was like a long winding road. For a long time, the joy and excitement when it was good, won over the downs. It developed its own traction. I tried to keep myself busy doing courses, changing jobs and organizing holidays. But I was lonely.

I reached my limit at some point. It was time to clear things up once and for all and to set the record straight – were we in or were we out. If we were in, then I wanted some reaction from Rosa as to her place as an Aspie in our family and my place as the Neuro-typical. If we were out, I wanted her out of the house. Either way I felt it would be difficult.

By that time, I had given birth to Ben my son and he was three years old. Rosa was besotted with him. She wanted our family to stick together. I understood her point of view, because I knew that for her, institutions were important. They gave her security and a sense of order and purpose. But our relationship had been getting worse and worse and the family was not going well, for me.

We had had several episodes in which we had come to blows. I didn't want Ben to grow up in that environment and I didn't want it for myself.

I remember one chilly autumn evening in our little house in Collserola. Collserola is the National Reserve that surrounds Barcelona and prevents it from spreading indefinitely into the pine forests and beyond. It is a safe haven for birds, wild pigs, and other forest animals and people who want to live close to nature. There is a limited urbanized area and beyond that is the park full of pines and holm oaks, cistus and viburnum, llentiscle and fennel, growing wild. The autumn in Barcelona is chilly but the summer heat still lingers and makes it gentle.

It was Autumn time. We had all gone to bed. Rosa had fallen asleep with Ben, and I left them snoozing together. I left a window open for our four cats. Alfi the grey tiger striped daddy, needed to come and go. Crawling out of bed a 2 am to open a window to Alf's incessant scratching to come in and half an hour later to let him out, again, was more than I could bear. I snuggled down with Storm and floated into a doze. Rosa woke up and found the window open. We had a thing about windows. I heard her from the living room next door, "Tsk, tsk, that woman…" The level of tension after years of this kind of conflict was about 10,000 on the Richter scale. My body stiffened and I lay there trying to contain myself. I couldn't. I stormed out of the bedroom and re-opened the window.

"What the hell are you doing, we'll all freeze to death."

"No, we won't and you're not the one who always gets up for the cats, you're usually snoring."

"I'm not having the windows open. Ben will catch pneumonia."

Recalling our therapy sessions, I consciously avoided sneering and sarcasm, but the venom was there, behind my eyes and oozing out of every pore.

"No, he won't, he's tucked up."

"Yes, he bloody will."

"Let's go into the kitchen and close the door so he won't hear us and wake up."

"OK."

Things escalated. Rosa's eyes narrowed and her face seemed to turn black as her muscles jerked. I pushed her and we were fighting on the kitchen floor. Suddenly a pain shot through my hand and the battle was over. Something bad had happened to my left index finger. The same one as Rosa had broken years ago. We drew back like fighting cocks, still furious, but taken aback now. It might be broken I muttered and slunk off to Ben's bedroom to snuggle up to him for comfort. He was fast asleep.

The house was silent and in the end, I got up to go to the kitchen again. Rosa sat crumpled in a kitchen chair. Her head hung down and she stared at the floor.

"See how it is tomorrow," she whispered, "I knew I'd done something. I knew it would hurt."

"We can't do this anymore."

"No."

My finger wasn't broken but it was an injury that took two years to heal.

In a strange way, everything had happened as it should. I couldn't have left the windows closed. Rosa couldn't have expressed irritation without blowing up. We were both, playing with dynamite.

I found it ironic that when there was just me and Rosa, it had been me putting the effort in to make the relationship go. Now that there was Ben and I felt less lonely and more secure in myself, I wasn't so concerned about the relationship. On the other hand, Rosa had become more attached.

We continued to row and make up and row and make up and I had the idea that separate rooms might help. Maybe having two spaces would have calmed things down because it was obvious that we had different needs sometimes and no way of communicating them in a meaningful, operative way. The needs seemed to be the source of a lot of our fights. However, Rosa couldn't imagine this idea as useful and that caused yet more friction.

You may wonder what kept us together. There were fascinating conversations about all kinds of things, a basic similarity in morals and ethics and a mutual love and respect for animals. I think we could see the value in each other but just couldn't quite reach into the heart of the matter.

The Good

We had some wonderous times, usually on our own. Going for meals together was always one of our favorite pastimes. We enjoyed discovering restaurants, choosing food and eating out together. It was where we had our best conversations and I liked watching Rosa over a table. It was comforting and relaxing. She was an excellent date and made me feel as though I was the most important person in the world. But Rosa was like that with everyone. People adored her because she had a gift for making each one, feel like the only one. She was as generous and charming and captivating with everyone.

We had safaris in Kenya that didn't come from a package tour. We drove up and down the country and through game parks in a way that people don't do anymore. Rosa, an excellent driver, would pick up any hirecar, anywhere and get it on the road.

Our first safari in Kenya was with a friend of ours, Ceci. Three "girls," we were set on "doing" Kenya independently. Hiring a Rav4 with camping equipment, I drew up a route. I had lived in Kenya as a child and knew the place, somewhat. We were a bit like "Thelma and Louise," plus one. Trekking through the game parks, and through tiny roadside villages. I tried to map out routes off the beaten track but we soon found it wasn't necessary. In Kenya, the beaten track was wild enough.

My two partners in adventure were marvelously game and made the most of every moment. Rosa was the chief driver, although we all shared. Ceci was a good general all-rounder and peace-keeper. I navigated.

Driving out of Nairobi on our first morning, Rosa at the wheel, grinning like silly monkeys, we reveled in the energy. Thrilling at the sight of the rich red earth, muddy from recent rains and the fresh scent of ozone, we left the city behind. Lush vegetation and the barefoot children in school uniform, hurrying along the roadside to school kept us chatting loudly. Tiny three-year olds with older brothers and sisters made us wonder at their freedom and independence. We had taken a bag full of pens and pencils and stopped to hand them to the cold little outstretched hands. It was chilly after the rain and the children were scantily dressed. Children surrounded the car like tiny fishes on a piece of bread. We marveled at the joy that such a small thing could give. We were on an Africa trip high, and more so because we had fixed it all ourselves.

Rosa spotted an old man lying in one of the deep muddy ditches by the roadside and wanted to help. She stopped the car again and got out. As she approached the old guy, Ceci and I stared as the man rose up from the mud and lurched toward Rosa waving his big stick aggressively. A cyclist rescued her, telling the old geezer to simmer down. He was very drunk.

Rosa felt compelled to help when she saw road accidents or any other kind of mishap.

My routes took us outrageously off road at times and Rosa drove on. I had chosen a route to get to Olorgasailie. Olorgasailie is the birthplace of humanity and is in Maasai territory. I was determined not to take the main road, which would have led us into Nairobi. As our RAV4, loaded with camping equipment, gingerly edged down a dried riverbed full of huge boulders, I realized there was no need to look for off road routes, in Kenya. This road was marked on the map as a decent secondary road. After a long while of not seeing a soul, we began to spot the odd Maasai dressed in traditional dress. At one point, a man in a smart suit with a briefcase came picking his way over the boulders. He carried on past us, up the river. We stopped to ask two young Maasai girls how long we would take to get to our destination. They took a good long look at our four-wheel-drive, and with their heads tilted and long, delicate hands on their chins, "In this thing, two hours." We arrived almost exactly two hours later at the main road and the last lap of our journey. There was a local bar made of mud, where we stopped to get a much-needed Tusker.

I like to reminisce now, as it helps me to see that we really did have great times. I think on that particular trip, the combination of friends was perfect. Ceci was a mature woman with a very nice, tolerant nature, who was willing to see the best in everything, Rosa was focused and hungry for experience as long as she didn't have to initiate it and I was the insatiable traveler. We were together for three weeks; just enough, as the cracks were beginning to show towards the end.

At that time, I didn't know that Rosa had Asperger's syndrome and I would stop her and ask what was going on between us, on a regular basis. I often felt unsure of what she was thinking and feeling. I felt a little embarrassed about this, in front of our friend Ceci. I felt that a couple with a good relationship should be able to solve problems between them, discreetly. But between me and Rosa, discretion was, almost impossible.

Thoughts

I often mulled over the mystery that was Rosa. She and our relationship had become my main concern. Things like: life doesn't move on with her, time stands still, if I were on my own, I'd get my ass into gear and do so many more "things," so much more "stuff." Then came the thought, "But we've bought a house in Kenya, we've volunteered in an orphanage in Thika, we've bought a flat in Barcelona, she's helped me reconnect with my prodigal brother, she's shared Storm's life with me and loved her What more can a person want with a partner?" Then comes, "Emotional connection, support, understanding when there's no logical explanation for my tears, hugs when I need them, without having to ask for them…that's what I ask for."

We were moving on, we were working things out, we were beginning to understand each other, after 17 years. We could make it, it was all worthwhile and then, slam, bam, another meltdown, another fight, another crisis, another bout of madness. I was off again with, "This can't go on, I must leave, things never really change, I have to move on, life can be more fulfilling, I'm going to go mad, my heart is breaking, all I need is to be financially independent," and a whole lot more.

Asperger's syndrome is invisible to the naked eye, you have to have your Cassandra specs on the spot it. Cassandra was a beautiful priestess in Troy. Apollo fell in love with her at first sight and asked for a kiss. He said he would give her the gift of prophecy in she would humour him. She thought it was great fun and agreed. But just before the kiss, with Apollo's gift, she saw him helping to overthrow her city and spat angrily in his face. He couldn't take back his gift so he cursed her. No one would ever believe her prophecies. She predicted the fall of Troy, her city, and the way it would be taken. People with Asperger partners are sometimes called Cassandras because no one believes when they try to explain what it's like living with the syndrome.

Who Am I?

I am a sociable person and love to have folk in my house, proved it to myself time and again during my two-year stint doing Airbnb in Barcelona. Before I met Rosa, I used to dream of having just the relationship that I have and inviting my friends to enjoy and show off my home and happiness. What I could never have imagined was the sense of desperate, discontrol I had when people were round and Rosa was there.

Rosa had a different idea of friendship to me. Any new neighbors or acquaintances very quickly become old cronies. They were welcome at all hours to telephone or pop in, as long as she was the inviter. My intimate friends on the other hand, had strictly limited access.

We lived in a leafy neighborhood in a small town near Barcelona. We had some charming young neighbors and made friends with them. I need a little time, in fact a whole lot of time before I feel comfortable enough to have people round at any time of night or day for unlimited lengths of time. Rosa needs no time at all for this. She is happy to welcome practical strangers into our home at any time and for long periods of time.

I liked this young couple, Frencesca and Edu. They had some chickens in their little back yard. They had a small urban farming business and sold chicken coops and planters online. Edu was into computers.

Young chatty Francesca, with trendy glasses and stripy woollen tights would come over and outstay her welcome, nearly always. Edu, her handsome, goofy partner with unkempt black hair and thick inventors' glasses, knew when it was time to go.

At first, I enjoyed having them round for coffee. I liked having nice neighbors. But quite quickly, I began to feel the need to escape from Francesca. She would chat on about her stuff that I couldn't relate to. Rosa seemed to encourage her and all her inhibitions disappeared. Francesca felt unconditionally invited into our house. I would long to get away from her and my internal turmoil was much greater than the situation called for.

Rosa didn't understand my distress. She thought that Francesca was a bit pushy, but didn't suffer like me, so she couldn't help.

One evening, they were round at our house and time went by. I began to feel like I wanted my house back to myself. I wanted to prepare for bed or supper or something. There was no way of hinting subtly to anyone that I needed my home. I decided to take next doors dog for a walk, to get a break.

When I got back, the visitors were still there. So I crept into the neighbor's garden to take Dono the dog, home. I spied on my own home, through the fence. The inside of me was big and desperate. My stomach felt like it had a huge stone inside and my brain was murderous. I couldn't go home because I couldn't trust myself to behave well. I didn't want to humiliate myself by seeming inhospitable. I could just see the wary look on Rosa's face if I walked in and announced that it was time for them to go.

Eventually, I came back into my garden and hid in the tool shed, until Francesca and Edu had gone home, then, I exploded at Rosa. She had had no idea how much I had needed those people to go and there had been no way of letting her know. She had been totally absorbed in an interesting conversation with Edy. And Francesca had been happy to hang out.

Why had I felt so desperate? Probably because, there was no designated place in that house where I could go to be in peace, Rosa and I had no kind of understanding about moments like this and she wasn't able to sense my need on the spur of the moment. I had felt like the outsider and the weirdo in my own house.

My sense of "being ignored," by Rosa, in company, was so acute that the slightest discomfort felt enormous.

To be with anyone for long periods of time, it was important for me to have chosen the person especially or to have some kind of special, intimate connection with them. Otherwise, it was a huge effort. For me, socializing was not the same as having friends. It may be that I feel dreadfully unsociable but I want a friend at hand. On the other hand, it may be that I am enjoying being the good hostess, but haven't got time for my friends at a party. It seems that for Rosa, it is almost the opposite. She can spend hours with people she only vaguely knows but with anyone who is becoming more intimate, she had to establish some very strict limits.

Rosa couldn't stand last minute decisions of mine to have friends to stay. There were people who I made connections with and with whom there was a flow. Then, I might feel like inviting them to stay the night or for dinner. On this level, things just didn't go smoothly between us.

One evening we had been invited to a friend's wedding party. We were to meet some other mutual friends at our place and go together. These people came from quite far away by train and would have had difficulty getting home before the morning. I asked if they wanted to stay and then asked Rosa. They couldn't stay. Maybe I should have asked Rosa first.

I felt let down and empty. I didn't cause a fuss on the outside. But I wanted to be away from both Rosa and the friends. I hated myself for not being able to sort the situation out. All through the party I felt like I was moving through mud and it was an effort to make conversation. And when I did talk it was mostly about my bronchitis.

"So what are you doing here then," commented one guest. I couldn't think of a good reason.

Confusion

Why did I hold out so long for a relationship that caused me such grief I believe that some of my friends in whom I've confided over the years, saw my problems with Rosa as just an extension of my problems before her. And they a point and I took their point. Their advice was always to find my own interests and to be less dependent. They said, "Come and see us more often and to rely less on Rosa." This advice was valid, taking into account that Rosa had Asperger's syndrome. But nobody knew that at the time. Their advice stung, although I did try and follow it. I didn't find much comfort in my own efforts at independence. They didn't have the backing of anyone who really understood my situation. Just the same, I kept trying and trying and believing that if I could just reach that magic point of happy independence, I could be content. My whole life became a therapy to not feel lonely and misunderstood. Everything fitted in with my deep-seated belief that there was something wrong with me.

One big problem was that, whenever I really got close to anyone, Rosa would become furiously jealous. She couldn't see me laughing, drinking, hugging or playing with anyone where she couldn't understand the context. I would find myself torn between Rosa and my new found friend. It happened about three times in our relationship as far as I can remember, with real, practical consequences.

I had a lot of reasons for continuing the relationship with Rosa. She was my first serious relationship that had started at the age of 38. She was a fine person and I knew it. There were amazing times between our meltdowns. I loved her crazily, "She gives me love, love, love, love crazy love," could have been our song if we had ever shared an emotional connection to a song. She kept me guessing. Things never went stale. They couldn't, because Rosa didn't keep emotional stuff in her head. It was intoxicating.

The good times were mind blowing and so were the bad times. The cocktail of emotions had me hooked. After every fight, the reunion was like a honeymoon. I don't mean sex. The sentiments were fresh and romantic. I would daydream again about our perfect future. I planned our dream home and the next trip to Kenya. This was all as real as the sleepless nights when Rosa was off on a meltdown and I was hopeless. And there was always just enough of my dreams come true. We got our house in Kenya, we went on trips. There was enough to keep me going.

Conversations were pretty interesting too. As long as I steered clear of emotions, we could talk for ages. Since Rosa doesn't sift information, she would bring her stories of the hospital home in their raw state. She was an anesthetist, so she was in at the ground floor of emergencies, heart and brain surgery and broken legs.

"I was really pissed with Sonia, today, she took an hour doing an op that should have taken her 10 minutes just to piss Justin off."

"What!" I exclaimed mouth hanging open in indignant disbelief.

"Yeah she's a real nitwit."

"Who, Sonia?"

"Of course, she made me late."

"And the patient, what about the patient!?"

"Clara, I really like your take on things."

We kept each other interested.

Blind

Our relationship had what I called blind spots. It had always had them, from the beginning before I even knew about Asperger's Syndrome. I knew there was something a little odd about the way we dealt with conflicts. We never managed to reach that point. The Richter scale would rise from 0 to 10 in seconds. Neither of us knew how to stop. I thought of these instants before full scale battle broke out, as blind spots. When you are driving, you can see almost every angle from the driver's seat but there are always those few inches that are completely invisible. No matter which angle you look from, you can't see what's coming. Rosa and I could talk in retrospect, on an intellectual basis about what had happened,6 and we could analyze, scientifically how to try and prevent the explosion, till the cows came home. But there was always a blind spot. There was always an area which one of us couldn't see, a spot that our vision didn't quite hit. It was always there. The question was, could we ever learn to be careful enough to avoid the crashes?

We didn't. We crashed in Spain, we crashed in England, we crashed in Australia, we crashed in Kenya and all the way to Norway and back. The only place we didn't crash was in Hong Kong under the benevolent eye of Rusty my beloved stepfather, where I felt safe. There was no conflict there.

The crashes were spectacular and the debris, sad. There would be days of semi-silence, overcast with fear and pain after the crash. It took me ages to realize that if I came round more quickly, Rosa would follow.

Making Sense

It is hard to believe that the amazingly good things ever happened between us. There was no emotional back-up, when it was bad, there was no evidence that it had ever been good. When it was good, there was no recognition of the glitch. Our relationship sometimes seemed like a wasteland, although rationally, I "know" what we did. I'll make a list, Rosa liked lists.

We got together:

- lived together
- bought a lovely old attic flat in Barcelona and did it up together
- travelled all over western Europe up to Norway with my cat Stormy, in a Peugeot Partner, together
- re-found my prodigal brother together
- met Rosa's friends and family
- moved out of Barcelona into the country
- travelled to Kenya regularly together and supported an orphanage and hospital there
- bought a house in Mombasa
- had a baby

Soooo, why the wasteland effect? It feels like I either did it all alone or else against Rosa's wishes. Soooo, why was she physically at my side, most of the time? I think it's because we both had very different agendas.

For me, the bad times lingered, and it was hard for me to wipe out their memory. For Rosa, when we were at peace, they were all gone, all better.

Also, for me the good times lingered, when she was in a meltdown and the relationship was over. I couldn't swallow it. There were still traces of love and tenderness.

For me, things had an aftermath, and for her, they didn't.

It was a bit like the difference between a computer and a notebook. Once something is deleted from the computer, it's gone but if something is written in a notebook in ink, it lasts for a very long time, it's there even if the notebook is lost. Rosa was the computer, and I was the notebook. Even if I consciously erased something in order to carry on, it was there somewhere skittering around my brain.

Rosa loved me but I was not the center of her world. I tried to make myself the center of her world.

Doctor

When we moved out of Barcelona into a little ground floor apartment in a pretty town near Barcelona, things were okay for a while. Rosa's work wasn't too far away and I had a bit of gardening work, which I loved. We both liked the house and in ourselves and individually we were contented. We each established our own routine and lived fairly peaceably, circling each other. It was at this time that we bought our house in Kenya. This was my desire and Rosi was happy to support my dreams financially, as long as they didn't interrupt her routines and professional plans. She was working on her thesis. She came to some important conclusions right out of the blue, Einstein style, while suffering from a head cold at the beach in Mombasa.

We had some good holidays in Kenya and even went volunteering together. Rosa became involved in carrying ex-hospital supplies to Kenyan hospitals. She did a week's stint, volunteering in a busy township hospital, completely off her own bat. Looking back, she was and still is quite amazing. She filled suitcases with syringes, bandages, tubes and other surgical supplies and we turned up at the hospital to donate them. I acted as translator, as in Kenya they speak English. After 17 years with me, Rosa didn't speak English.

She was deeply humbled and impressed at the quality of medical care offered and the level of expertise of the doctors, in spite of crushingly low funds.

I was in awe and admiration of everyone involved in this magical episode. Rosa really was quite spectacular sometimes, she had superpowers.

We went back the following year with an old but working defibrillator, for the hospital. We got it there on the back of a bicycle-taxi.

So, what was our problem? Why did I feel so desperately lonely and unseen all the time? Why did Rosa need to disappear for a night leaving me bereft whenever I tried to raise the subject of our imperfect relationship? We obviously felt passionate about each other and about quite a few important things in common. There was no question of anything fizzling out.

Revealing

During the early years of our relationship, I made friends with a woman called Giselle. The friendship was brief because she had reason to want to cut off relations with all friends of her ex and I was one. I had enjoyed talking to her and she had seemed a wise and funny person.

Giselle was large and lovely. Her voluptuousness proved too much for our lesbian friend Dani who was Giselle's first woman. Her piercing dark eyes would stare down into mine with amusement. We made a connection and talked a lot. At the end of her relationship with Dani, we sat one long summer afternoon on her rooftop terrace chewing over their affair. She was very intelligent and loved a philosophical challenge. But Dani had broken her heart.

Years later quite by chance we met again, while I was gardening. The woman who owned the garden mentioned that Giselle was living there. I was cautious about meeting her again. I wasn't sure that Jane would be happy to see me. One day she appeared, walking up the garden steps, a half-smile on her face. As she approached me, my body relaxed and I smiled back. It was as if no time had passed.

We became quite close again and I talked to her a lot about me and Rosa. She listened and offered moral support.

She seemed to understand me. I had a level of desperation, sometimes, when Rosa went off, that was quite unbearable, and seemingly out of proportion I would talk to my analyst and would literally wear out my various friends' ears, until they could no longer understand what I was going on about.

One day when I was feeling distraught, I called Giselle and she invited me round to go for a walk with her, her son and their dog. We walked amongst the dusty pines and through the hills of the beautiful Collserola national park, where we lived. I described my experiences and feelings of desperation at the repeated abandonments and returns. I told her that I could make no sense of the fact that I stayed with this woman even though she hurt me deeply time after time and seemed to feel no remorse or even realize the effect of what she did. I described my delight in her when we were alone together and feeling cozy. I described how Rosa would walk out on arguments before they even began, leaving no scope for reaching an agreement, leaving me in a state of desperation, feeling bereft. I described my own special states of feeling abandoned and Rosa walking out was like torture to me. I explained how a couple of times she had promised not to walk out again but didn't keep her promise. I told how I, kind of, believed Rosa did this to hurt me but how I always felt there was something more detached behind it.

Giselle recognized things in what I said and told me that it sounded similar to her experience with a man she had had a relationship with. This man had a thing called Asperger's syndrome. Then she explained what this was and I recognized things too.

As the pieces began to fall into place like a puzzle, it was like a page being turned in a mystery story. I started to grin a little guiltily as I realized that I was discovering something about Rosa, without her. I wanted to shout it to the world that I'd sorted out the mystery of our relationship. But at the same time, I knew that I was still with Rosa and she was the other half.

My thoughts raced but in slow motion as if on a screen and not in my own head. Two different things, what I could do with this information and what Rosa would do with it. There were a million moments explained in one. I saw with breath taking clarity how things had happened. Then I thought of Rosa and how I knew her. She would take a lot longer to see.

I went home feelings cautiously hopeful that Rosa and I had a chance of making things better and that I had a chance of a happier life with her.

In actual fact, the whole process of revelation was deeply complicated, a minefield of prejudices and blame.

The first thing I did was to borrow a book from Giselle about a little boy who developed an understanding with his nanny. I think the book is "Isaac's Cup". The story is a true one about a little boy with autism whose mum finds him the ideal nanny. The nanny is a young woman with Asperger's syndrome. She can understand the boy better than anyone else. In the book, the mum tells of the friendship between the three of them and the magic that happened.

The book points out that a lot of people have "shadow autism." I wondered if I had a bit of that too. "Shadow autism" is when a person has some of the traits of autism that manifest very subtly. Someone who always feels awkward at parties for example, may have shadow autism. A person who finds it hard to open up to relationships, may also have shadow autism. The phenomenon is quite common.

I was getting in the mood for talking to Rosa. I felt that if I could tell her that I could relate to her and not blame her, maybe I could reach her. I thought that telling her this would lower barriers and help us. Talking to Rosa was never the difficult part. Getting a response was more complicated.

When I mentioned all this to Rosa, she looked at me and said "Maybe." I jiggled about a bit and tried, "Interesting, isn't it?"

"Mmm, yeah, do we need to do a shop?" I left it there until I could speak to Jane, which was far more satisfying.

The next thing I remember, was playing around with a book with Asperger's tests at Jane's house. Rosa played along and scored high and then went for a nap. She wasn't interested. Jane and I were much more worked up and did the test too. We scored pretty low and nodded knowingly to each other.

We juggled ideas: me and Rosa were unique, possibly the first case of AS found in a lesbian couple, Rosa was fascinating, we could start an AS community in Spain. We got ourselves well pumped about it. Grinning at each other, we discussed conferences, diagnosis, Rosa giving talks and Maxine Aston coming to do a workshop. This was all great in theory. But I had the gnawing sensation that the jamboree that Giselle and I were cooking up was very different from what was going to happen between me and Rosa. I knew Rosa, Aspie or not. She wasn't very psychologically inclined I glanced over at her snoring on a sun lounger and had a sinking feeling.

I let the fun, the air of friendly conspiracy with Giselle make me feel as if I had something to get my teeth into. The trouble was that when I thought about Rosa, I knew that it would be complicated. But with typical Sagittarian optimism, I threw myself into this new project of "fixing us." Again, the trouble was that the other "fixer" was my friend and not my partner. Rosa was willing to comply as long as it was just a game. She thought the tests amusing and interesting at best, at worst an invasion of her privacy. Her point of view was perfectly valid but I was so anxious to get to the bottom of all this and find that bit of peace and happiness for me and Rosa, that I could just perceive at the end of the rainbow, if only… The "and Rosa" bit, was a mistake.

Rosa did agree to a diagnosis and that more or less was that. I began to see that we would never form part of the twosome, working on life together, that I had been incubating in my dreams. I was always uncertain about what was in store for us. And discovering Asperger's syndrome, didn't change that basic truth. We loved each other, there was no doubt about that. I admired Rosa immensely and could see her trying from her position of AS, every day to love me how I wanted.

From my point of view, the discovery wasn't the answer to any puzzle. The puzzle went on. Why did no one, absolutely no one I know, except Giselle, and including my family want to talk to me about this? Why if I had made the great and wise discovery of a problem that does seem to have answers for others, are there none for me? My analyst was very good in her field and had been listening to me talk about me and Rosa for years. When I told her about Asperger's syndrome and Rosa, she said, "But she can't have AS, she's an anesthetist." This woman was very clever and a good psychologist. My friend Shaun's reaction was that I shouldn't say such things about Rosa behind her back. My friend Gill just gave me a funny look and turned her back on me. What is sooo bad about Asperger's syndrome? Nothing, intrinsically, as far as I can see apart from the isolation and loneliness it brings.

Rosa seemed to me, to accept our condition just as it was and didn't feel any need to work anything out or to modify our daily life to accommodate this addition to our family.

Me and Rosa lived in Spain and were a couple of married lesbians. Rosa was "out" in her hospital. I consider this pretty liberal for a still basically catholic country. But any sign of psychological unusualness would have been more than her job was worth. "Oh, that I lived in Australia!" I sometimes thought after reading some literature on the subject, where the AS experts live. That would be another story Jackanory.

Baby

In 2010, we were living in Valldoreix, in the valley, just over the Collserola range that forms the national park surrounding Barcelona. Our life was settled and we'd been together for 12 years.

After discovering the AS element in our relationship and realizing that there wasn't going to be a, 'Eurika', moment with tearful thanks, I began to feel very restless. Things with Rosa didn't change much but I began to morph inside. I needed something in my life and it had to be big. A house in Africa wasn't enough.

There was still a yawning emotional gap in my life. Courses and gardening and even yearly visits to Kenya couldn't fill it. I would weep under the steamy, hot water of the shower. Rosa knew this.

"Are you going to cry again."

"Yes."

"Oh, OK."

I comforted myself with walks through the pines with the neighbor's dog, Dono. We made friends and his owners were happy to have me take him out. Greeting other dog owners along the way, I felt more cheerful.

My mind wandered just like my feet. Young people passed me by. More and more I noticed them and began to think. I'd had an abortion in London in about 1992 and believed that I didn't want any babies.

When we were all around 40, some of my single girlfriends quickly got themselves pregnant. I hadn't caught the baby bug then. But 10 years later, I couldn't get the idea out of my head. "These young people could be my children." I thought time after time, as Bono and I ambled through the woods. I had plenty of spare time to day dream. Rosa had a good steady job to support us both. I did as many gardening jobs as I could get. But I had never had a vocation.

I mentioned it to Rosa. She told me to talk to her gynecologist friend, Susana. I was a little taken aback but did so. Susana told me exactly what to do to get pregnant at age 50.

"Susana! Hi, look, I'm wondering about having a baby."

"Mmmmm, do you still have your period?"

"Yes."

"You're pretty young and healthy for your age, so it should be okay. I'd say you need an implant. You see your eggs are pretty old and it wouldn't be a good idea try for a baby with them."

"Wow, really, that simple."

"Yes, you know the baby won't have your DNA, but I don't think that will be a problem, will it?"

"Nooo, no, no, I'd just be delighted to get pregnant."

"Right, well, you think it over, but quickly. Get back to me and we'll get to work."

"Wow, thanks Susana. Oh, and is it going to be expensive?"

"No it's really cheap, 2000 Euros for the whole treatment."

"I can really do that!"

I thought for a month on holiday in Kenya. While I thought, Rosa and I continued to fuss and fight as always. I had a conversation with Giselle, over the telephone at one point.

"And what about getting pregnant, Clara? Would you do that without Rosa?"

"Yes, that has nothing to do with us. If I have a baby, it's my decision."

When I got back, I rang Susana again and we began to get me pregnant.

An implant means that an embryo, resulting from another couple's IVF treatment, is placed carefully into the (fertile, throbbing, hungry, swollen, rich, bloody, eagerly waiting) uterus of the woman receiving the implant.

In Spain, the woman who has IVF treatment has the right to decide the fate of her extra embryos. She can donate them to a laboratory, have them destroyed, keep them for herself for later or donate them to other women. I was the beneficiary of one woman's generosity. The donors remain anonymous, and the doctor fits the embryo as nearly as possible to the characteristics of the birth mother.

Susana got me well souped up with hormones for two weeks, before doing the implant. I had never imagined so many hormones could be inserted into my up and down orifices. I reeked of female hormones. It felt like I was just lying around like a fat queen bee, waiting for her drones. In fact, I carried on gardening and walking Dono as normal.

The day of the implant dawned, and Rosa and I set off for the private clinic, early in the morning Rosa had arranged to work in the afternoon that day as she was getting interested by then. The smart building and air of affluence that private clinics give off made me feel confident. A friendly receptionist pointed the way to the reproduction department. The nurse showed me to a private room and asked me to get undressed and lie on the bed. I noticed the wall light at the head of the bed and a set of scales and grimaced inwardly at my nakedness under the hospital gown. Rosa looked on quietly commenting on hospital equipment.

A pleasant looking man in a blue overall came in and explained that they would implant two embryos. I listened smiling and thanked him. Then a nurse came and took me to the surgery. There was a gynecologist with a computer screen in front of him.

"I can see everything that's going on inside to guide Susana when she does the implant."

"Susana's coming then?"

In she walked in hospital scrubs. I couldn't see her mouth but her eyes were kind.

"You won't feel a thing."

I was immediately on the alert. When a doctor says that, you can guarantee that there's something to feel.

"Well now," chimed in the one on the computer, "it is a bit uncomfortable Su."

Susana just eyed him. It was uncomfortable. But it was over very quickly. The nurse came to wheel me out to the resting room where I had to stay a while.

"Now love, if it doesn't work the first time, don't get upset, you can always come back."

I just grinned at her. I already knew I was pregnant. The question was…with one or two?

Ben was born by emergency cesarean and Rosa was the first to hold him. I was splayed out on an operating table, my arms in crucifix position to stop me trying to touch anything. The attending gynecologist was stitching up both the caesarian slit and the episiotomy she had seen fit to perform, without warning me and without anesthetic. Rosa was so incensed with the clumsiness of the delivery that my doula had to remind her she had a newborn baby in her arms. Ben commented, "UGGG!" looking up at her face, and Rosa became besotted.

I imagined we could be a happy, if eccentric, family. I still believed that Rosa and I could offer different types of love and caring to Ben and that we would find a way to sort out our violent rows.

Cassandra

I was a Cassandra. No one believed how mind blowing it was living with someone with Asperger's Syndrome. Deep down I knew this when I discovered it and wanted to scream, "Hey, something is going on here!"

I told various people and each time shriveled a bit more like a stranded worm on a scorching day. The only one who would listen was Giselle and that caused tension between me and Rosa.

Ironically, Rosa became my only ally in my campaign to sort out the enigma of AS. She didn't mind listening to my discoveries, from reading books. But she wasn't interested in acting on any of them.

I begged her to go see Maxine Aston who had diagnosed her. I thought that if she could just understand that there was no blame, she could somehow change. I was still hopeful.

One evening, when I was exhausted from being with my baby, I spotted her reclining in front of the telly. I transformed from a tired mum into a raging wild cat.

"Rosa, I want you to go and see Maxine."

"Aw not that again, why, what's the point if you tell me I can't change."

"You can't change but maybe you can learn something about Asperger's syndrome."

"I've read the books."

She doesn't speak English; all the books I had bought were in English. Rosa's reading habits had always puzzled me. She told me that she read pages in diagonal and could glean the information she needed in seconds. I accepted her claim to have read the books in English without questioning. But I was foxed.

"Well, why don't you write to her, if you don't want to see her."

I had gleaned that people with Asperger's syndrome like communicating in writing better than talking.

"Aw no, I don't want to."

"Rosa just do it."

"No I'm not going to."

"Just bloody do it!"

"No!"

Then I understood what meltdown was. My mind seized. I think I wept. I could see only one way forward and it was blocked. I became obsessed with her seeing Maxine. In the end, about two years later, she went.

I decided to go and see Giselle, who lived in Scotland by then. Ben was six months old and we went for two weeks. Rosa later said that when she saw us off at the airport she went back to the car and wept over one of Ben's dirty nappies.

I couldn't understand how she could love us and at the same time refuse to do anything to make things easier.

Sadness

We stayed together for a long time after my "discovery" and life went on much the same as before the "discovery". Rosa was Rosa and I was me. No 'Aha' moments or, 'Thank you darling for discovering the mystery of our troubles.'

On a trip to Kenya in 2015, we stayed in the house that we had bought there. We knew before going that it might not be easy to spend a month on holiday together. By that time, I was wondering how much longer I could carry on. But I had bought the tickets in one of our jolly moments and we couldn't bear to waste them. Ben was with us, of course. The month was very difficult. We were neither separated nor good lovers any6more.

Most of the time, Rosa holed up in a separate room with her tablet and android. It was the only way we could avoid coming to blows. Over what? You might want to know. In my case, basically my frustration that Rosa refused to recognize how Asperger's affected our relationship, since I found out about it six years before. When things went wrong, she looked at every possibility outside the relationship and other than her and came up with some pretty convincing theories: my mother had ruined me for relationships, my work was not going well so I was fed up and the latest was that little Ben was exhausting me and I was out of my box. Well, there was, annoyingly, an element to truth in all those observations. BUT also, there was an element of Rosa that was responsible for my discomfort. My listening skills, by then, had diminished.

After three weeks in the same house, we had had a few tender moments but in general we were like two fighting cats again. I had made the mistake of painting the room that Rosa was occupying, and she had had to move out, into my room, because of the smell. She was very sensitive to certain sounds and smells. I knew that paint was a strong smell but wasn't thinking straight.

She spent her last night in our house on a wicker recliner with a few cushions just outside my door. You don't go looking for a hotel in rural Kenya, especially without a car, after dark. Anyway, I still couldn't leave her alone. When my goat is got, it doesn't go away easily. She was in tears as well as furious and she asked me, "How can you chuck a person who has to get up at 6:30 to go to work every day out of the house on a winter's night, with nowhere to go?" I had done this various times in the last year. I must say in my own defense that if I hadn't chucked her out, she would have gone anyway. She couldn't stand the heat of my anger. Rosa stayed till dawn and then left.

How can I have done that, I ask myself. She was right. How could anyone who thinks of themselves as decent have done that? All I can say is that in my relationship with Rosa, I have thrown to the winds almost all my preconceptions of how decent people behave towards each other. When we 'fought', there were almost no holds barred and that was one of the very practical problems that I faced. Rosa didn't face it; she didn't see it, in retrospect. Fought, is in inverted commas because even that was outside anything that I could have imagined. There was no argument as such and very little dialogue. There were insults, which I and quite a lot of threats but the actual reason for the beginning of the trouble, always, became hard to track.

Later on, we were in Kenya again, still, limping along together. We had had the same night watchman for all the years we had the house, about eight. Suddenly, Rosa took to disliking him. I liked him. He had heard us argue and shout and had advised us to quiet down, as it's not good for neighbors to hear trouble in the middle of the Kenya night, in the middle of nowhere. It makes the place vulnerable. He had seen a lot with us and there was plenty of fuel for resentment. And he would snore on our veranda. This made Rosa apoplectic.

We were uncomfortable in the house, and I would wander around in the night. Sometimes I would cry. Sometimes I would sit on the veranda in the middle of the night and talk with David. One sleepless night I had drifted to the veranda. I was startled when David asked if he could help me with biological matters. I was a bit hazy about what he meant and just said no thanks. Later I mentioned this to Rosa, in one of our good moments and we laughed a bit. I wasn't 100% sure that he meant what I thought he might have meant. But, when Rosa began to despise David, the memory of this, added rocket fuel to the putrid cocktail of resentments.

One night, things came to a head. I was restless again and wandering around and Rosa was tense. She appeared out of the dark and headed for the tool room and grabbed a djembe (hand hoe). She screamed at David, who was sitting on a bench in the back garden in the dark, "Get out of my house, you miserable little turd." I wasn't having it so I stormed out telling the man to stay put. I couldn't understand how things had come to this. Little Ben called out and I went for him. I couldn't behave like an adult and just go back to bed and let things calm down. I carried Ben out to our caretaker's little house and crumpled on one of his tatty armchairs. His family must have been listening through the thin walls of their bedrooms, but they didn't stir.

David retreated to the tiny damp, dark space between the outside and inside gates to the road. It was the space officially meant for the night watchman. He stayed there all night, peering through the spy hole, inwards, not out. Later, he told me he had never been humiliated by a woman before. Kenyan men have a lot of pride.

Later, Rosa joked that now Stuart the caretaker, and David knew what it was like to get a western woman going in a bad way. I didn't find it funny. I just felt very sad and my crying in the night got worse.

End

In the end, we separated. The process was long and slow and there was no moment of decision. There was no period of mourning either. In a way the family continued to function.

Rosa moved to our flat in the city and I stayed in our house in the hills surrounding Barcelona. Ben went to primary school near there and Rosa saw him at weekends.

I continued to hurt for quite a long time. I made the decision to separate. Rosa wanted her family, even though the good times had mostly gone. The extraordinary thing is that Rosa was still there for me in a practical sense. She still paid the bills and the rent. And we still spent some weekends together.

Little by little the relationship developed into some kind of friendship. Unsteadily and shakily, we wrote our own story. The story goes on and I think it will forever because with Asperger's syndrome, there is no beginning, middle and end.

Post Data

As I have hinted, my story with Rosa is not over. I think that as a couple, we have finished our race. Now we are working on friendship and sharing Ben. I believed that by "finishing" with Rosa, I would cut a huge chunk of tension out of my life. This hasn't really been the case. Because we have Ben and are still married, everything is still very emotional. Emotions in a relationship with someone with AS, are a nuisance.

Rosa is still on board for any future plans I concoct, and I still imagine her there somewhere in my life.

My life with Rosa was wonderful. She dragged me kicking and screaming out of my past and into the present. I had had big issues before, I met her, and she allowed me to work them out. I still have issues* but discovering someone with Asperger' syndrome was also discovering myself.

I would like my story to resonate with other people who have lived intimately with Asperger's syndrome. It has been a privilege for me to know Rosa. The fact that I found the relationship with her difficult was not one person's fault. Amazing things happened and we both loved and we both wanted to be loved. We both benefitted and suffered.
I believe that any relationship with a lover, is a case of "It takes two to tango." In relationships, we can grow and learn.

www.ingramcontent.com/pod-product-compliance
Lightning Source LLC
Chambersburg PA
CBHW070659250726

48662CB00001B/197